The Best of
KANSAI
KYOTO • OSAKA • KOBE

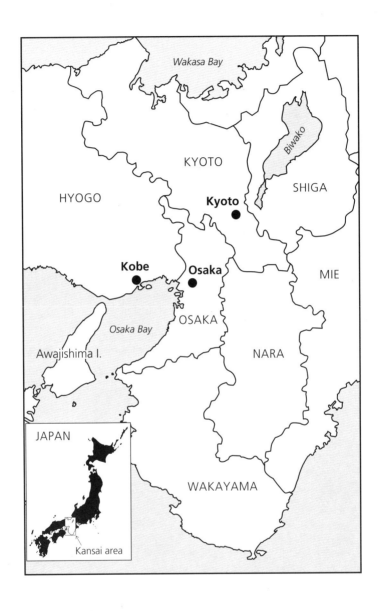

The Best of
KANSAI
KYOTO • OSAKA • KOBE

John Frederick Ashburne

Tuttle Publishing
Boston • Rutland, Vermont • Tokyo

Published by Tuttle Publishing

© 1998 by Charles E. Tuttle Co., Inc.

All rights reserved

Library of Congress Catalog Card No. 97-60050
ISBN 0-8048-2069-4

First printing, 1998
Second printing, 2000

Printed in Singapore

Distributors
Asia Pacific
Berkeley Books Pte. Ltd.,
5 Little Road #08-01, Singapore 536983

Japan
Tuttle Publishing
RK Building 2nd Floor
2-13-10 Shimo-Meguro
Meguro-ku, Tokyo 153 0064

North America, Latin America and Europe
Tuttle Publishing
Distribution Center
Airport Industrial Park
364 Innovation Drive
North Clarendon, VT 05759-9436

For Steve Day
who would have loved Japan,
and SJA
who undoubtedly did,
and for Sasha
who helped more than she knows.
Kampai!

Contents

Introduction *13*

Restaurants *17*
  Best Airhead Cafe   19
  Best All-You-Can-Eat-Sushi   20
  Best Authentic French Cuisine   21
  Best Averagely Stupid Noodles   22
  Best Brazilian Coffee   24
  Best Budget Taiwanese   24
  Best Budget Thai   25
  Best Bulldog Ramen   26
  Best Cave Ramen   27
  Best Cheap Eats   28
  Best Chicken   29
  Best Coffee and Dog   30
  Best Garlic Restaurant   32
  Best Healthy Ramen Lunch   33
  Best Healthy Viking Lunch   34
  Best Hida Cuisine   34

Best Kyoto Station Food   35
Best Luxury Chinese   37
Best Noodle/Bath Combination   38
Best Okonomiyaki Internet Cafe   39
Best Rough-and-Ready Sushi   40
Best Rude Food   41
Best Soba   42
Best Tea—Green   43
Best Tofu Restaurant   45
Best Traditional Chinese   46
Best Umeda Station Food   47
Best Vietnamese   48
Best White Rabbit Noodles   50
Best Wild Boar and Bath   51

Sights **53**
Best Advice—Tourist   55
Best Back-to-the-Future Airport Train   56
Best Bath   57
Best Darumas   58
Best Day Trip from Osaka   58
Best Early Morning Meditation   59
Best Edo-Period Erotica   60
Best Fashion Museum   63
Best First Date   64
Best Geisha Watching   65
Best Giants Gas Station   66
Best Glitz Palace   67
Best Hidden Temple   68
Best Hot Spring Hideaway   69
Best Hot Water—Outdoor   70
Best International Toilets   71
Best Map of Kyoto and Nara   72
Best Nerd Watching   73

Best Peace Museum   74
Best Photography   75
Best Rainy Day Out   76
Best Secluded Garden   77
Best Sleep   77
Best Tourist Temple   78
Best Yakuza Watching   79

Bars *81*
Best Bourbon with a Bite   83
Best Candlelit Nightcap   84
Best Classic Stand-up Boozer   85
Best Cozy Late-Night Cocktails   87
Best Metalhead Bar   88
Best Microbrewery   89
Best-Named Bar   90
Best Reggae Cave Izakaya   91
Best Shutterbug Bar   92

Entertainment *95*
Best AAAArgh!   97
Best Cinema   98
Best Discount Tickets   99
Best Elvis   100
Best Fire Festival   101
Best Free Movies   102
Best French Movies   103
Best Gay Cinema   104
Best Library   105
Best Live House   106
Best Oops Upside Your Head   107
Best Place to Shoot Your Friends   108
Best Reggae Warehouse   109
Best Stand-Up-and-Do-Your-Thing   110

Best Tunes   111
Best Video Rental   112
Best What's On   113
Best Whips and Chains   114

Shopping 115
Best Antique Street   117
Best Art Supplies   120
Best Art Books—Japanese   121
Best Art Books—Western   123
Best Beatles Memorabilia   124
Best Bicycles by Post   125
Best Books on Old Japan   125
Best Coffee Beans   126
Best Everything-Under-One-Roof   127
Best Ex-Kimonos   128
Best Familiar Drugs   129
Best Flea Market   130
Best Free Furniture   132
Best Handcrafted Furniture   132
Best Handmade Shirts   134
Best Impulse Buying   134
Best Japanese Paper   136
Best Luxury Kitchenware   137
Best Mail-Order Everything   138
Best Male Members   139
Best Mineral Water   139
Best Pepper   140
Best Pickles and Goblins   142
Best Plastic Food   143
Best Secondhand Books   144
Best Secondhand Cameras   145
Best Secondhand Macs   146
Best Wine Retailer   146

Services *149*

Best Advice—Legal 151
Best Cat Sitters 152
Best Change Machine 153
Best Dentist 153
Best Environmentalists 154
Best Home Massage 155
Best Hospital 156
Best Human Rights Resource 157
Best Internet Service Provider 157
Best Nose Job 158
Best Travel Agent 159

Index of Entries and Addresses in Japanese *161*

Index by Area *171*

Note: On the maps that appear throughout this book, hyphens have been kept to a minimum. To aid the reader, hyphens are used more frequently in the text.

Most of the photographs in this book were taken by the author.

Introduction

Five centuries ago, when Tokyo was merely a festering swampland populated by ruffians, unscrupulous money-grabbers, and ne'er-do-wells of the most heinous variety (unlike today, of course), Western Japan was the undisputed cradle of Japanese culture and civilization. Or, at least, it was where all the rich people lived. The Kansai aristocracy would engage in such lordly pursuits as moon-gazing, writing poetry, and subjugating the poor, but above all they loved two things: partying, and telling everyone else how great they were. Little has changed today. As any right-thinking, level-headed Kansai-dweller will readily tell you—and they will very readily tell you—this is the real Japan, the cream, the nectar, the blissful hypocrene. (Hyperbole, along with karaoke and eating octopus balls, is a local pastime). Kansai's temples are more beautiful, its gardens more sublime, its cuisine more sophisticated, and its octopus balls more, well, ballsy.

Kansai is huge—its GNP is greater than Canada's—but

it's also accessible. It takes less than half a day to travel from the virgin forests of Ashiu in the north (complete with wild bears and long lizards) to the decidedly non-virgin bars and clubs of Osaka's Shinsaibashi (with wildlife of a different kind). Kobe is just fifty-five minutes from Kyoto by express train. In addition to its large size, Kansai is blessed with variety. While the locals enthuse about the region's unique character, each of its four cities is quite different. Kyoto, the best known of the four, has some of the oldest and most beautiful temples in all of Japan, fantastic restaurants, theaters, and much more. On the surface, Osaka, the region's economic powerhouse, is all business, but underneath it's shameless, sleepless, and very, very, loud; Kobe is trendy, cosmopolitan and, despite its tragic recent history, full of vitality and optimism; and Nara, the region's forgotten cousin, is a place to chill out and be at peace.

In this book, I've attempted to capture the best of this lively region, the place I now call home. What do I mean by "the best"? Certainly not the best known, or the most popular, and definitely not the cheapest. One cold winter's afternoon, as I sat with friends by the window of my Japanese house, we hit upon the following definition (aided by a few glasses of saké): an "amalgam of excellence and style, infused with dashes of fashion, wit, and good taste, washed down with healthy doses of irreverence and personal prejudice." A few glasses later we also decided that we like places that don't cost an arm and a leg, and that you can reach by bus. By the end of the bottle, we were down to "anywhere we'd had a really good time."

One learns as one writes. For all the nasty things I've said about Kyoto's occasional aloofness, I've come to realize that it's still my favorite city, and as such, is heavily represented in these pages. I can't resist the endless maze of coffee shops, galleries, trendy bars, and student-filled restaurants. Its back streets are an unhurried tourist's paradise. Oh yes, and the temples are okay, too. Where once I hated Osaka for its look-alike streets and non-stop hustle, now I have to admit to a grudging affection for its unbridled *joie-de-vivre,* its earsplitting bars, and its who-gives-a-damn-anyway attitude. It reminds me of Florida on amphetamines. If people seriously dress like that, the city can't be all bad. Then there's Kobe. I've always liked this wonderful port city, a kind of Liverpool with prettier girls that's full of Chinese restaurants, Jain temples, reggae clubs, boomerang superstores, and all the erstwhile paraphernalia of a genuinely international city. I like it even more as it fights back from the cataclysmic Great Kansai Earthquake of 1995. (If only the earthquake had waited a while and hit the new Kyoto station complex instead!)

This book is meant to start arguments, not settle them. To better reflect the fact that I've either discovered or been introduced to many of the places mentioned in this book by friends and colleagues, the first-person plural "we" is used in the descriptions throughout. We hope that you'll try out these places, experiences, and services in a critical but balanced frame of mind, and then discover we were right. Or, if not, that you'll have a great time trying to prove us wrong.

restaurants

Restaurants

BEST AIRHEAD CAFE

Minden, Osaka Prefecture
Suita-shi, Esaka-cho 1-23-10, Daido Seimei Bldg., 2F.
Tel. (06) 385-6978. Mon.–Fri. 8:00 A.M.–6:30 P.M.; Sat. 8:00 A.M.–2:00 P.M. Closed Sundays and holidays.

Our very first images of Japan, gleaned in the early sixties from a black-and-white BBC TV documentary, were of Tokyo policemen wearing anti-smog masks, and pale, half-asphyxiated office workers plugging into vending machines for a breath of (bottled) fresh air. Which goes to show that *"le plus ça change, le plus c'est la même chose,"* and all that. Some thirty-odd years later Suita's greenest coffee shop, Minden, offers ten minutes of oxygen inhalation in addition to coffee and herb tea. For ¥450 (¥350, if you're planning on drinking coffee afterward), you get to experience the sensation of *shinrinyoku* or "breathing in the forest." We cannot help but admit to feeling mightily stupid donning the oxygen mask in front of hordes of highly amused office ladies, but we cared not, for Minden fits another, important *Best of Kansai* category—Best Hangover Cure. Nice plants, too.

ACCESS: Midosuji Line subway to Esaka station. Leave the train at the front exit, turn right, and the Daido Seimei Building is directly in front of you.

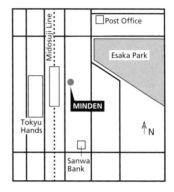

BEST ALL-YOU-CAN-EAT SUSHI

Yumezushi, Osaka
Higashi Osaka-shi, Nagata Naka 3-1-91, Grand Maison Higuchi, 1F.
Tel. (06) 744-7079. 10:30 A.M.–10:00 P.M. Closed Mondays.

Sushi paradise. All the eel, salmon, cod roe, sea urchin, and more that you can cram down for ¥1,000. Choose from over 50 different types of sushi. What's more, there's no time limit. Not surprisingly, this place gets packed with fish lovers. Expect a wait of up to 30 minutes on the weekends.

ACCESS: Chuo Line subway to Nagata station. Leave the only exit and walk west as far as the Tokai Bank, then turn north and walk along Route 2. After two blocks, Yumezushi is on the southeast corner.

Best Authentic French

Bordeaux, Kyoto
Kyoto-shi, Kita-ku, Omiya Gentaku Minamimachi 35-5. Tel. (075) 491-4743/492-6901. Fax. (075) 493-7779. Lunch 11:30 A.M.–3:00 P.M. (Last order 2:30 P.M.) Dinner 5:00 P.M.–10:00 P.M. (Last order 9:00 P.M.) Closed Mondays. English and French spoken. All major credit cards accepted.

Kansai "French" restaurants are more plentiful than dozing pigeons on the Eiffel Tower, but finding Le Real McCoy is akin to coaxing a belly-laugh from a Parisian. Bordeaux, perched high on a hill overlooking north Kyoto, is a notable exception, where even the mirrored walls and Louis XIV furniture appear to have been transplanted directly from Les Halles or Montmartre. This writer has found that even the most Westernized Japanese chefs usually fail dismally when they try to recreate true Italian cuisine, but their Francophile counterparts often seem to outdo their Gallic teachers. Bordeaux's owner and chef, Takao Omizo, is a case in point, and his years spent studying in the city for which his restaurant is named are evident in every dish. Takao is proud that his food is "wholly French," and he openly pours scorn on restaurants that lace their menus with sashimi to cater to Japanese tastes. Not surprisingly, authenticity comes at a price, with set menus ranging from the reasonable to the lavish (¥6,000 to ¥20,000). We recommend that you tell Takao-san your budget in advance, and let him decide your *menu de degustation*. Incidentally, Takao-san told us this is where George Lucas and the Duke of Kent stop by "when they are fed up with raw things."

22 THE BEST OF KANSAI

ACCESS: Six minutes by taxi from Kitaoji subway station. Alternatively, take Bus no. 6 from Shijo Omiya station, or Bus Kita 1 from the Kitaoji bus terminal. It's a one-minute walk from the Tsuchitenjocho bus stop, opposite the Koetsu Jidosha Kyoshujo driving school.

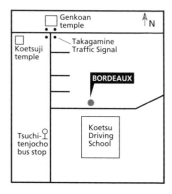

BEST AVERAGELY STUPID NOODLES

Bongu, Osaka
Osaka-shi, Taisho-ku, Izuo-cho 4-4-7.
Tel. (06) 553-7272. Thursdays to Sundays. 11:00 A.M.–4:00 P.M., or until the noodles are gone, which is inevitably before 4:00 P.M.

The name of this restaurant means "Averagely Stupid." Yet there's nothing average about this superb noodle restaurant, tucked away in a former art gallery in Osaka's Taisho-ku. The decor is tasteful, from the *soba*-slurping elephant on the signboard outside, to the hand-carved furniture and superb red-clay porcelain bowls within, and the unreservedly warm welcome from the staff, but it's the magnificent *soba* that keeps us coming back here time and time again. On our first visit we ordered the *hosogiri soba,* (¥900), thinly sliced and cold, served with the simplest but deepest of dipping sauces, and considered it some of the best we'd ever eaten. Until, that is, we followed it with the incredible duck and spring onion *kamojiru soba* (¥1,200). Served in traditional Tokyo Edo-mae style, with the noodles cold and a hot dipping sauce alongside, the *kamojiru soba* left us speechless with satisfaction. We recommend you are liberal with the *sansho* seasoning, and accompany it with some cold Amano saké.

Once upon a time, Bongu would have been the only reason to visit this suburban part of the city, but of late Taisho-ku has been undergoing a quiet renaissance. Galleries, antique shops, and ethnic eateries have been springing up everywhere, prompted in part by the large influx of residents from Okinawa, a cheery bunch given to throwing impromptu street parties in very non-Japanese fashion. Check out the Okinawan foodstuffs shop, **Pepino** (Tel. 06-552-5225), or the makeshift and very popular **Chai Kobo** (Tel. 06-552-5225). Taisho-ku's most recent eye-catching addition is the enormous Osaka Dome. (See Best Place to Shoot Your Friends.)

ACCESS: A fifteen-minute walk from Taisho station on the JR Kanjo-sen loop line and the Nagahori Tsurumi Ryokuchi Line subway. Walk along Taisho-dori, until you pass under the Hanshin Kosoku expressway. Bongu is down the second street to the right off Taisho-dori. Look for Mercury Video shop on the corner. Bus nos. 70 and 71 from Namba Kabukiza Ura bus terminal to Minami-Izuo.

BEST BRAZILIAN COFFEE

Cafe Zinho, Kyoto
*Kyoto-shi, Sakyo-ku, Shimogamo Nishi-Honmachi 37.
Tel. (075) 712-5477. 9:00 A.M.–midnight. Open every day.
English spoken. No credit cards.*

This gem of a cafe offers the best coffee this side of Rio, plus real Brazilian snacks, sandwiches stuffed with ham and cheese, and hair-raising alcoholic Caipirina cocktails, all at cheap, cheap prices. Owner Mori-san loves to talk about his beloved Brazil unless, that is, he's slumped behind the counter in one of his many impromptu siestas. Even the sublime espresso (¥200) cannot keep him awake. The cheap and tasty food keeps us coming back for more. Take note of the great notice board, too.

ACCESS: City buses to the junction of Shimogamo Hondori and Kitaoji-dori, on the south side of Kitaoji.

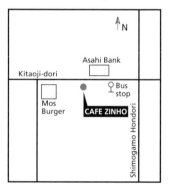

BEST BUDGET TAIWANESE

Aa Ri Shan, Kyoto
*Kyoto-shi, Shimogyo-ku, Shijo Muromachi Kado 2.
Tel. (075) 212-8155. Mon.–Fri. 5:00 P.M.–10:00 P.M., Sat, Sun, holidays 4:00 P.M.–10:00 P.M. Open everyday. All major credit cards accepted.*

This is a hugely successful budget Taiwanese restaurant that has evolved into an even more successful chain. After you try the cuisine here, you'll realize why their success is so well deserved—inexpensive, tasty, with speedy, friendly service.

ACCESS: On Muromachi-dori, a two-minute walk northwest from Shijo subway station and Hankyu Karasuma station.

BEST BUDGET THAI

E-san, Kyoto
Kyoto-shi, Kamigyo-ku, Imadegawa-dori, Karasuma Nishi Iru, Imadegawa-cho 325.
Tel. (075) 441-6199. 11:00 A.M.–2:00 P.M., 5:00 P.M.–10:00 P.M. Closed Sundays. English spoken. Visa cards only.

When the *tom yam kun* and *tom kha gai* cravings kick in, but the wallet remains sadly empty, head for E-san. Thai restaurants have sprung up by the dozen of late in Kansai, but this tiny Kyoto restaurant sitting just across the street from Doshisha University is the most authentic and economical of the bunch. The menu is huge, the service a little slow (but friendly), and the helpings are always generous. Spending ¥2,000 per head will leave you replete. The ¥5,000 dinner set for two includes five dishes plus dessert—the best-value-for-money Thai food this side of Khaosan Road.

ACCESS: Imadegawa subway station, or bus nos. 59, 201, or 203 to the junction of Karasuma-dori and Imadegawa-dori. E-san is the second building (to the west) on the north side of Imadegawa-dori.

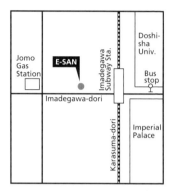

BEST BULLDOG RAMEN

Tahiti, Kyoto
Kyoto-shi, Kamigyo-ku, Senbon Kuramaguchi, Higashi Iru Hitosujime.
Tel. (075) 431-7517. Noon–midnight. Closed Wednesdays.
No credit cards.

No, not in the noodles. It's in the kitchen where Boo-chan, the owner's bulldog, drools appreciatively over this top-class *ramen*, with its heavy, deep and garlicky taste. Strictly for meat-eating dog-lovers. The *kizami-niku* beef *ramen* is outstanding. The *gyoza* and fried chicken are also local favorites.

ACCESS: A five-minute walk east along Kuramaguchi-dori from Senbon-dori, just back on a narrow side street to the north. Look for the flashing red and banana-yellow sign.

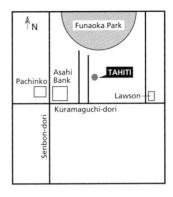

BEST CAVE RAMEN

Yosuko, Osaka
Osaka-shi, Kita-ku, Kakuda-cho 7-17, Toho OSM Bldg., 1F. Tel. (06) 312-6700. 11:00 A.M.–10:50 P.M. Closed second and fourth Thursdays. No credit cards.

The *ramen* shop by which all others should be judged. Light, non-oily *assari* clam soup with a deep, flavorful taste, garnished with *kikuna* vegetables, served in a classic Chinese setting replete with stone armchairs and a shiny aluminum counter. It really would have the feel of a cool cave restaurant somewhere in Szechwan, were it not for the salarymen crowding in at the door. Cheap, too. *Ramen* from ¥450, and *gyoza* only ¥200. No alcohol served. They also have original souvenir ramen packs, as sold in Takashimaya and Hankyu department stores, for ¥450. Owner Nakazawa-san started Yosuko twenty years ago and their popularity remains undiminished. Essential Kansai eating!

ACCESS: Hankyu, JR, or Hanshin lines to Umeda station. Behind Navio department store, in the alleyway in front of the OS Gekijo theater.

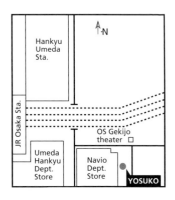

BEST CHEAP EATS

Daigin, Kyoto
Kyoto-shi, Sakyo-ku, Jodoji Higashida 60.
Tel. (075) 751-7890. 11:00 A.M.–10:00 P.M. Closed Thursdays.
No credit cards.

Kyoto is notorious for the expense of even its cheapest restaurants, so it comes as some surprise to find west Japan's best cheap eatery here, and in an upmarket neighborhood to boot. Just a stone's throw from Ginkakuji temple and the start of the Philosopher's Walk, Daigin has an exhaustive range of cheap and delicious *teishoku* (set meal) dishes. Either choose from the menu or point out what you want from the dishes displayed in the glass case by the door. Large servings.

ACCESS: Bus nos. 5, 11, 203, or 204 to Ginkakuji-michi. Daigin is just east of the intersection of Imadegawa-dori and Shirakawa-dori.

Best Chicken

Toridori, Kyoto
Kyoto-shi, Kamigyo-ku, Imadegawa Chienokoin Sagaru Tel. (075) 411-8788. 5:00 P.M.–10:00 P.M. Closed Thursdays. No credit cards.

For most of us meat-eating Westerners, the humble *niwatori,* whether it be Au Vin, Kiev, or Colonel Sanders, is a species to be consumed just one way—well and truly cooked. No such limitations apply at Kyoto's Toridori, where sashimi takes pride of place on the menu. The Tottori-born owner, Koji Miyaji, is nothing if not creative. The raw chicken is actually rather good, especially the *sasami bainiku,* chicken breast with Japanese plum sauce (¥500) and the *tori sarada,* chicken salad (¥500). A mug of chicken soup is both breathtakingly good and cheap (¥200), but best of all are the *tsukune* meatballs: have them fried (¥500) or steamed (¥400), or served *agedashi*-style with soup (¥500). The former are so good we have double helpings every time we visit. Also outstanding is the *yuba tsutsumi,* a sublime combination of minced chicken, beefsteak leaf, and mushrooms with *yuba* bean-curd (¥700). Toridori was established just two years ago, and the woodwork still smells fresh and clean. Mr. and Mrs. Miyaji don't speak English, but their unpretentious welcome applies in any language.

ACCESS: Just 100 meters south of the junction of Imadegawa-dori and Chienokoin-dori. Bus nos. 52, 201, or 203: Get off at Jofukuji bus stop and walk east along Imadegawa-dori until you reach Chienokoin-dori.

BEST COFFEE AND DOG

Doji House, Kyoto
Kyoto-shi, Kita-ku, Koyamamoto-cho 20-21.
Tel. (075) 491-3422. Noon–11:00 P.M. Closed Thursdays.
English spoken. No credit cards.

This coffee shop is named after its star attraction and, many would argue, the real owner of the place: Doji, the golden retriever. Doji visits each individual table, and bestows a quick nuzzle on favored customers, while his master rustles up Western-style salads in the kitchen.

RESTAURANTS 31

ACCESS: Subway to Kitaoji station. Walk north along the bank of the Kamogawa river to Kitayama-dori and turn left. Doji House is on the north side of Kitayama-dori.

Best Garlic Restaurant

Ninnikuya, Kobe

Kobe-shi, Chuo-ku, Nakayamate-dori 2-13-1, Landmark Bldg. Kobe, 5F.
Tel. (078) 271-3838. Mon.–Thurs. 5:00 P.M.–midnight.
Fri.–Sun. 5:00 P.M.–3:00 A.M. Open every day. English menu.
All major credit cards accepted.

My imagination had conjured up garlic milkshakes, garlic mousse, and other such culinary grotesqueries, but the food at Kobe's Ninnikuya, the House of Garlic, is surprisingly gentle on the palate. Rest assured that their fare is neither weird nor outrageously pungent. Capitalizing on the success of its Ebisu, Tokyo forerunner, Ninnikuya is currently one of the most popular eateries in post-quake Kobe. Even for a mid-week visit, reservations are recommended for this anything-as-long-as-it's-cooked-with-garlic eatery. We especially liked the *gyuniku-tataki* raw beef with garlic (¥1,200), and the simple, but dazzling fried garlic. Large portions, served with great night views across Sannomiya.

ACCESS: A five-minute walk uphill from Sannomiya, on the west side of Hunter-zaka just beyond Nakayamate-dori.

BEST HEALTHY RAMEN LUNCH

Galando, Kyoto
Kyoto-shi, Sakyo-ku, Tanaka, Furukawa-cho 37. Tel. (075) 712-4581. Mon.–Sat., noon–4:00 P.M. Fri., 6:00 P.M.–8:00 P.M. Closed Sundays and holidays. No credit cards.

Galando is a most relaxing east Kyoto lunch stopover. Run as a cooperative by a group of Hanazono University graduates, it serves healthy, Japanese lunch sets (always with a vegetarian option) at very reasonable prices. In the best Kyoto student tradition, they give wall space to a variety of environmental and politically worthy causes, and we especially like the fact that they employ staff with disabilities. We are addicted to Galando's *tonkatsu* ramen, which not only tastes great but is actually healthy, an unlikely combination that we find as irresistible as it is unlikely; despite our best intentions we rarely manage to order anything else. Upstairs, there is a non-pedagogic "cram school" where children are encouraged, of all the outrageous things, to have fun and play. In Kyoto dialect, Galando means "empty space," something this nice little restaurant is unlikely to have.

ACCESS: A two-minute walk west of Chayama station on the Eizan Dentetsu Line, or bus no. 206 to Tanaka Okubo-cho.

Best Healthy Viking Lunch

Obanzai, Kyoto
Kyoto-shi, Nakagyo-ku, Koromonotana-dori, Oike Agaru. Tel. (075) 223-6623. 11:00 A.M.–2:00 P.M., and 5:00 P.M.–9:00 P.M. Lunch: Mon.–Fri. ¥810; Sat., Sun., holidays ¥1,030. Dinner: ¥2,030. Open every day. No credit cards.

Although they are open into the evening, the real bargain at this central Kyoto organic restaurant is the "Viking-style" all-you-can-eat lunch. The menu runs to mostly vegetarian Japanese-style fare. The restaurant seats 60, but as this place soon fills with Nishijin clerical workers and office staff, it's best to arrive early.

ACCESS: Subway to Oike station, exit 2. Walk three blocks west of Karasuma, then 100 meters north of Oike on Koromonotana-dori. About a five-minute walk.

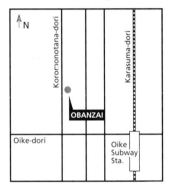

Best Hida Cuisine

Daruma, Kobe
Kobe-shi, Chuo-ku, Nakayamate-dori 1-16-3. Tel. (078) 331-2446. 5:00 P.M.–10:30 P.M. Closed Sundays and holidays. English spoken. Credit cards accepted.

Daruma is a cozy downtown Kobe retreat specializing in cuisine from the Hida region around Takayama in Gifu, an area noted for its fresh mountain vegetables and grilled miso soybean paste. The walls are adorned with paintings and illustrations of Daruma (famed Buddhist saint), including one large artwork painted by an American Zen priest. Recommended are the assorted *sansai* mountain vegetables, the charcoal-grilled *yakitori* chicken, and the eponymous *hoba-yaki,* miso with vegetables grilled on a *hoba* leaf atop a small brazier, a snip at ¥500. Wash it down with the sublime Hida-Takayama saké. About ¥2,000 per person.

ACCESS: Hankyu or JR lines to Sannomiya station. On a small street leading east off Higashimonsuji-dori, south of Nakayamate-dori.

BEST KYOTO STATION FOOD

Izakaya Tengu, Kyoto
Kyoto-shi, Higashiyama-ku, Shichijo-dori, Kawabata Minami Sagaru.
Tel. (075) 561-2146. From 5 P.M. till closing. Open every day. English spoken. No credit cards.

We pity the poor souls who pack into McDonald's on Kawabata-dori, unaware of the warm welcome awaiting them next door at Izakaya Tengu, surely south Kyoto's most welcoming eatery. The food is standard *izakaya* fare, but it's cheap, tasty, and made with the freshest ingredients, bought daily at the nearby Chuo Ichiba (Central Market). The *niku-jaga* stewed beef and *yakizakana* grilled fish are especially recommended. But what really distinguishes this place is the warmth of its owners, the cheerily good-natured Mama, Batchan, and the hilariously effusive Master, whose back-slapping beer-quaffing style soon identifies him as a native of central Osaka. Tengu is actually a six or seven-minute walk east of Kyoto station, but anything on offer in the glitzy new station complex pales beside Tengu's simple, homey charm. Handy for visitors to Sanjusan-gendo and Higashi Honganji temples, the great secluded garden Kikokutei, and the *yakuza*-watching areas of Shichijo. However, Tengu opens in the early evening, a few hours after the temples close.

ACCESS: Beside the southeast exit of the Keihan Line Shichijo station, next door to McDonald's, at the junction of Kawabata and Shichijo-dori. Six or seven-minute walk east and slightly north of Kyoto station.

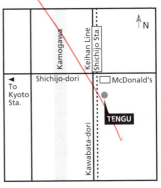

Best Luxury Chinese

Mr. Hal, Kyoto
Kyoto-shi, Nakagyo-ku, Karasuma-dori, Rokkaku Sagaru, Karasuma Plaza 21, B1.
Tel. (075) 241-6039. 11:30 A.M.–2:00 P.M., 5:00 P.M.–10:00 P.M. Open every day. Holidays vary. Reservations recommended.

Gilt mirrors, acres of starched white tablecloths, and waiters who pounce at your every whim. Not everyone's cup of tea, but for that special occasion, Mr. Hal just can't be beaten. Lunch courses start from ¥2,500, but if you've come this far you should push the boat out for an evening extravaganza. Budget for ¥10,000 per person. The Beijing-style cuisine is excellent, the decor and ambience lifted straight from Europe.

ACCESS: Hankyu Line or subway to Shijo-Karasuma station, exit 21. Walk north for five minutes.

Best Noodle/Bath Combination

Hatsuneya/Hatsune Onsen, Kyoto
Kyoto-shi, Kita-ku, Oyama Hatsune-cho 15.
Hatsuneya: *Tel. (075) 492-9191. 6:00 P.M.–2:00 A.M. Closed Thursdays.*
Hatsune Onsen: *Tel. (075) 492-4827. 3:00 p.m.–2:00 A.M. Closed Thursdays.*

In a sense, this must be the quintessential Japanese experience—a great bath, followed by great food. Downstairs, Hatsune Onsen offers scalding water, a sauna bath, and lots of gentlemen with full-body tattoos (¥320 entry fee); upstairs the *sento*-owner's son, Shigetaka Higashide, serves up exquisite *soba* and *udon* noodles in a trendy, art-bedecked restaurant. Inexpensive. The *ume udon* (¥650) is simple and sublime.

ACCESS: Subway to Kitaoji station, exit to Imamiya-dori—a five-minute walk west.

Best Okonomiyaki Internet Cafe

San-kichi, Osaka
Osaka-shi, Fukushima-ku, Ebie 1-1-23.
Tel. (06) 457-0935. 11:00 A.M.–9:30 P.M. Open every day.
URL: http://www.izutsuya.com/sankichi.index.html

It could only happen in Osaka, where the pancake-like dish is exalted to godlike status on a par with the Hanshin Tigers baseball team and, er, octopus balls. Access to the Internet is free, as is the coffee. Only one computer available. "Modan-yaki" becomes "modem-yaki"?

ACCESS: Hanshin railway to Noda station. Sankichi is inside Noda Jusco department store, on the fourth floor.

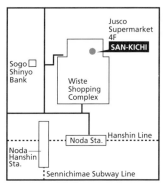

BEST ROUGH-AND-READY SUSHI

Yamanizushi, Kyoto
Kyoto-shi, Kamigyo-ku, Senbon Shimodachiuri Kado. Tel. (075) 801-4436. 5:00 P.M.–1:00 A.M. Closed Wednesdays. English spoken. No credit cards.

As splendid and good-looking a *sushiya* as you'll find in Gion, but don't let the appearance mislead you. Inside the staff yell and shout, presided over by the ever-beaming master, while the customers yell and shout too, washing down the excellent sushi with tankards of foaming ale. This is where the city's working men come to splurge, giving the place a cheery unpretentious vitality. A welcome change from Kyoto's infamous reserve. The sushi is top rate and inexpensive. About ¥2,500 per person.

ACCESS: A two-minute walk north from the junction of Marutamachi-dori and Senbon-dori. Bus nos. 55 or 201.

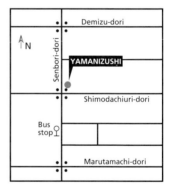

Best Rude Food

Dojo, Osaka
Juso Honten: Osaka-shi, Yodogawa-ku, Juso Honmachi 1-7-4, Plaza Pao, 1F.
Tel. (06) 308-1313. Mon.–Sat. 5:00 P.M.–2:00 A.M.; Sun. and holidays 5:00 P.M.–12:00 P.M. Open every day. Reservations recommended.

Who on earth would want to eat at a restaurant wholly dedicated to filthy lavatorial humor and third-rate schoolboy innuendoes? Most of the people we know, actually. This is the gastronomic equivalent of a National Lampoon movie, the menu liberally scattered with cucumbers, bananas, "testicle tomatoes," and other variously phallic, or suggestive ingredients. The whopper sausage is known as "The Gaijin," something we felt secretly good about, until one of our significant others coolly suggested that it was probably nothing more than a wiener with two new potatoes. Ouch! The Minamikata branch (Tel. 06-309-8649) has the totally disgusting *itteshimatta* sausage. Rude pictures on the walls, silly fun, and the cheapest date in Osaka in every sense of the word.

ACCESS: A three-minute walk from the west exit of Hankyu Juso station, one block west of the Juso branch of the Sumitomo Bank.

Best Soba

Furusato, Hyogo Prefecture
Hyogo-ken, Kinosaki-gun, Takeno-machi, Tokose 864.
Tel. (0796) 48-0435. From 11:00 A.M. Irregular holidays.
Reservations recommended.

We take our buckwheat noodles most seriously indeed, and thus this category was by far the most difficult entry to provide. Mouthwateringly excellent *soba* shops abound in Kansai's urban centers, but we've decided to ditch logic, and recommend Furusato, a noodle shop so far off the beaten track that only the true devotee would bother seeking it out. One of a handful of restaurants nestled in the remote *soba*-making village of Tokose in northern Hyogo, Furusato is more than just a noodle restaurant: It is the quintessential soba experience. The riverside setting is perfect and the noodles are far tastier than their much-vaunted rivals in Izushi, the soba tourist town at the foot of Mount Kannabe. Customers dine in this traditional farmhouse at *irori* hearths, eating first *soba,* and then charcoal-grilled yamame river fish, or the fresh mountain shiitake mushrooms for which the region is duly famous. This is simple, sublime country cuisine at its best. Autumn is when the noodles are the finest, but in winter don your snow tires, luxuriate in front of the charcoal fires, and warm up with a flask of the locally brewed saké. Budget ¥2,500 per person. Best to call in advance, in Japanese, for reservations.

If you've made it this far you might as well stay overnight and take in the paragliding school at Up Kannabe, the ski-slope at Oku Kannabe, the crab restaurants and hot-spring baths of Kinosaki, or the manmade (but still rather inviting) Kannabe Yunomori Yutorogi hot spring (Tel. 0796-45-1515).

ACCESS: Approximately three hours by car from Kyoto on Route 9, then Route 312. Follow the signs for Kannabe Kogen, climb the mountain from Ebara to Hidaka-cho and Ota village, then drop down the other side of the mountain to Tokose. A much more roundabout route is to take the train to Takeno on the San-in Line, then catch one of the infrequent buses to Tokose.

BEST TEA—GREEN

Ippodo, Kyoto
Kyoto-shi, Nakagyo-ku, Teramachi Nijo Kita.
Tel. (075) 211-3421. 9:00 A.M.–7:00 P.M. Closed Sundays.
Credit cards accepted. English spoken.

Once official suppliers of tea to the imperial family, the folks of Ippodo have been selling the green stuff from their grand warehouse on Teramachi for the last 140 years. Choose from the traditional bright green *matcha,* the mellow sweet and fragrant *gyokuro,* the sharp and invigorating *sencha,* or the down-to-earth roasted *hojicha.* Recently, Ippodo opened a teahouse, **Kaboku,** inside the old building where you can enjoy a relaxing cup of exquisite tea for just a few hundred yen before heading back out to browse through the antique and art shops of Teramachi-dori.

44 THE BEST OF KANSAI

ACCESS: On Teramachi-dori, two blocks north of Kyoto City Hall. Bus to Kawaramachi Nijo, or a 15-minute walk from Keihan Sanjo station.

Best Tofu Restaurant

Tosai, Kyoto
Kyoto-shi, Nakagyo-ku, Takoyakushi-dori, Sakaimachi Higashi Iru.
Tel. (075) 213-2900. 5:00 P.M.–10:00 P.M. (Last order 9:30 P.M.). Closed Sundays and Mondays. Reservations recommended.

One of the great things about writing an opinionated guide is that you are allowed to recommend places with reservations, and Tosai is hugely recommendable, as long as one is prepared to put up with a few ifs, ands, or buts. Set in a magnificently restored old Kyoto house, Tosai embodies much that is Kyoto. It offers excellence and loads of refined *shibui* (cool and elegant) style—even if the service is a bit haughty and distant. The tofu cuisine is, without a shadow of a doubt, as superb as the setting. But expect to be turned away if you have forgotten to make a reservation, and if you do gain entry, expect to be surrounded by salarymen out to impress their friends, secretaries, or both. I suppose it all boils down to how much you love your tofu. We were distinctly impressed by the tofu *tsukuri-tate*, freshly made hot tofu with horseradish—add a little soy sauce for the full effect (¥320); the *yamaimo tanzaku bainiku-ae*, yam with sour plum sauce (¥400); and *namabushi to takenoko*, fish with young bamboo shoots (¥850). The *cheezu to tofu harumaki*, cheese and tofu spring rolls (¥620), were excellent too. Great food helps us forget that dyed-in-the-wool Kyoto reserve.

ACCESS: A five-minute walk northeast of Karasuma station (Hankyu Line) or Shijo station (subway), at the junction of Takoyakushi-dori and Sakai-machi-dori.

BEST TRADITIONAL CHINESE

Homai, Kyoto
Kyoto-shi, Kita-ku, Izumoji, Matsunoshita-cho 11.
Tel. (075) 231-5776. Noon–10:00 P.M. (Last order 7:30 P.M.)
Closed Mondays. No credit cards. Reservations recommended.

Authentic right down to its gray shoebox architecture, high ceilings, hexagonal tile floor, and the fearsome, yet friendly, don't-mess-with-me waitresses. The shark's fin soup is awesome. Spacious, but so popular, especially at weekend lunches, that it's best to call for reservations.

ACCESS: Subway or bus to the Kitaoji bus terminal, then east to the Kamogawa river. Turn south and walk for one block along the western bank of the Kamogawa to the first junction. Turn right and Homai is in front of you.

Best Umeda Station Food

Gataro, Osaka
Osaka-shi, Kita-ku, Shibata 1-chome 7-2.
Tel. (06) 373-1484. 4:00 P.M.–11:00 P.M. Closed third
Wednesday of the month. English spoken. No credit cards.

We stumbled upon this truly great *izakaya* in the Umeda station Kappa Yokocho by chance, attracted by the peculiar name—it's a dialect word for the Kappa watersprite—and the warm welcome of the Mama-san. What a serendipitous find it turned out to be. Gataro's cuisine is top-notch, while its prices are rock bottom. We especially recommend the *piri-piri daikon no gyuminchi* an almost nouvelle-cuisine combination of sliced radish and savory minced beef; the *yamaimo to kinoko no karashi mentaiko itame*, yam and *shimeji* mushrooms with a spicy cod-roe sauce; and the mouthwatering *hamo ume shiso* tempura, whitefish with sour plum and aromatic perilla in batter. The latter is a favorite summer dish in Osaka, and Gataro's is by far the best we've ever had—including that at restaurants five times the price. Try to get a seat at the counter to watch how the master runs the show with almost military precision—his small army of workers includes two coconut-coiffeured hip-hopping youths with the most seriously pierced ears in all of Osaka. The master himself is not without some "style" of his own. The last time we visited he wore a T-shirt proclaiming: Smile, and the world smiles with you; fart, and you stand alone. We smiled.

ACCESS: Chayamachi exit from Hankyu Umeda station. Walk through the antiquarian booksellers' arcade into the Kappa Yokocho bar and restaurant alley. Pass the Asian Kitchen restaurant, go past one small cross street, and Gataro is on the left.

Best Vietnamese

Mekong, Kobe
Kobe-shi, Higashi Nada-ku, Koyo-cho 5-15, Rokko Island, Market Scene River Mall West, 2F.
Tel. (078) 857-9222. 11:30 A.M.–3:00 P.M., 5:00 P.M.–10:00 P.M. (Last food order 9:30 P.M.) Open every day. English menu. All major credit cards accepted.

While Thai restaurants are fast becoming ubiquitous in this area, Mekong remains the only authentic Vietnamese restaurant in Kansai. Owner Mr. Tong made the mammoth journey from his home in Vietnam's Qui Non province some 24 years ago, fulfilling his dream of starting a restaurant three years ago when Mekong opened amid the gleaming high-rise apartments and shopping malls of Kobe's Rokko Island. The dream took a jolt when Tong lost his house, and much of his business, in the Great Hanshin Earthquake, but the customers are returning, lured by such delicacies as *mang tay cua,* crab and asparagus soup (¥800); *goi cuon,* those duly famous

Vietnamese spring rolls (¥900); *tom cuon thit,* Vietnamese shrimp tempura (¥1,000); *banh tet,* rice dumplings wrapped in banana leaves (¥900); and *banh xeo,* a Vietnamese equivalent of *okonomiyaki* made with turmeric and coconut milk (¥800). We stuffed ourselves with all the above, yet somehow managed to find room for *choi chien,* bananas flambéed in brandy (¥600), and washed down the meal with Saigon's 333 Beer (¥600) and *tra* tea (¥100). Though we'd just returned from a holiday in Vietnam and expected the tastes to have been adapted to suit the Japanese palate, we were not disappointed. Even the smiley, sleepy service is pure Vietnam.

ACCESS: A three-minute walk to the west of the Rokko Liner Island Center station, on the second floor of the Market Scene River Mall West Building, diagonally across from the Kyoto Bay Sheraton Hotel.

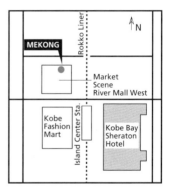

BEST WHITE RABBIT NOODLES

Mimi-U Honten, Osaka
Osaka-shi, Chuo-ku, Hirano-cho 4-chome.
Tel. (06) 231-5770. 10:30 A.M.–10:00 P.M. Closed Sundays.
All major credit cards accepted.

The noodles are white, but the rabbit is just in the name. The folks of Mimi-U (literally, the "Beautiful, Beautiful Rabbit") have been serving up unpretentious *udonsuki* noodle hot-pots since just after the war, and the popularity of their suitably warren-like noodle restaurant remains undiminished today. Mimi-U has branches in Tokyo, Nagoya, and Kyushu, but the original restaurant in the heart of Osaka's salaryman ghetto is by far the best. We went on a cold, wet October evening, which was perfect timing because by November the place is invariably booked solid. Mimi-U is the haunt of several Kansai celebrities, including the author Tanabe Seiko.

Can you bring yourself to plunge the still-wriggling prawn into the boiling soup? We had no qualms. Budget ¥3,000 per person, excluding drinks.

ACCESS: Exit 2 from Honmachi subway station. Turn left and walk along Midosuji-dori, past the huge Honganji temple, for five minutes, as far as the Norin Chuo Bank. Look for the Wariko digital clock above your head. Turn left here, and walk for two blocks. Mimi-U Honten is just down the street to the right.

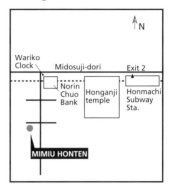

BEST WILD BOAR AND BATH

Iwaya, Hyogo Prefecture
Hyogo-ken, Taki-gun, Sasayama-cho, Hiuchiiwa 495-1. Tel. (0795) 52-0702. 11:00 A.M.–7:00 P.M. No holidays, but closed on the first and third Thursdays from April to September.

It's definitely worth a trip out to the wilds of Sasayama to partake of wild boar *botan nabe* and fresh mountain vegetables in this traditional country-farmhouse setting. Dine around *irori* hearths and have a post-prandial dip in the owner's *hinoki* cedar bathtub. The barbecue courses start at ¥3,500.

52 THE BEST OF KANSAI

ACCESS: JR Fukuchiyama line to Sasayama-guchi station. Bus to Hon-Sasayama, then another bus, marked Hiuchi-iwa Yuki, to Kogane-guchi.

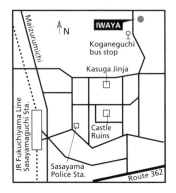

sights

Sights

BEST ADVICE—TOURIST

Tourist Information Center (TIC), Kyoto
 Kyoto-shi, Shimogyo-ku, Karasuma Shichijo Sagaru, Kyoto Tower Bldg., 1F.
 Tel. (075) 371-5649. Mon.–Fri. 9:00 A.M.–5:00 P.M., Sat. 9:00 A.M.–noon. Closed Sundays. Telephone information available every day.

That longtime foreign residents of Kansai still visit the Tourist Information Center is proof of their success at putting hapless foreigners in touch with whatever it is they need and desire. In addition to providing the best map of Kyoto, making event information available, and arranging accommodation—all in a variety of languages—they'll address more exotic demands. A beekeeper? Easy. An English-speaking Noh dance teacher? A cinch. A traditional Japanese inn that doesn't serve raw eggs for breakfast? They'll work on it. During busy periods, advising services are limited to five minutes per person. English, French, Spanish, Korean spoken.

ACCESS: Subway, JR, or Kintetsu lines to Kyoto station. On Karasuma-dori, ten meters north from Shionokoji-dori, directly beneath Kyoto Tower.

Best Back-to-the-Future Airport Train

Rapi><t, Osaka
Osaka-shi, Namba, Nankai Railway Information.
Tel. (0724) 56-6203.

Nankai railway's Rapi><t is a startlingly eye-catching machine, a thirties vision of the future that reminds us of Captain Nemo's Nautilus, Jules Verne's favored mode of undersea transportation. Not only is it cool-looking, it's by far the easiest way to get into Osaka. The non-stop Rapi><t Alpha makes the journey from Kansai International Airport to Nanba in 29 minutes. The slightly slower Rapi><t Beta stops at five stations, arriving in Namba in 35 minutes. Trains every 30 minutes, ¥1,370. Pity the poor Kyoto residents who have to make do with the plain-Jane, outrageously pricey JR Haruka.

Best Bath

Funaoka Onsen, Kyoto
Kyoto-shi, Kita-ku, Murasakino, Minami-Funaokamachi 82-1. Tel. (075) 441-3735. 3:00 P.M.–1:00 A.M. Closed Tuesdays.

This north Kyoto bathhouse opened in 1922 when it was designated a *tokushu yokujo*—a special bath—which entitled the owner to charge an especially high price for admittance. Today, the standard flat rate of ¥320 for a *sento,* or public bath, applies, but Funaoka Onsen is still a unique place. The changing room ceiling is dominated by a giant red-nosed *tengu* goblin, while the surrounding frieze depicts scenes of Taisho-era industry and warmongering, a stark contrast to the sense of peace and well-being you get from soaking in one of the seven baths. Just in case you get too relaxed, a stern-looking dragon spouts icy water onto your head in the cold outdoor *rotenburo* bath, and an even sterner *fudo myo-o* image guards over the hot outdoor bath. We particularly like the *kusuriburo,* a mysterious infusion of herbs which smells like celery, looks like boiling stewed tea, but leaves you feeling great. Afterward relax with a bottle of bright green milk or another of the odd-looking drinks that themselves seem like leftovers from a bygone age.

ACCESS: A five-minute walk east of Senbon-dori along Kuramaguchi-dori. A few minutes from Tahiti.

Best Darumas

Darumadera, Kyoto
Kyoto-shi, Kamigyo-ku, Shimono Shimodachiuri-dori, Onmae Nishi Iru Yukue-cho 457.
Tel. (075) 841-7878.

This quirky little temple is dedicated to everyone's favorite rotund red Buddhist saint, and is a haven of peace in Kyoto's Nishinokyo Enmachi. Check out the Daruma rooftiles, Daruma statues, Korean Daruma, female Daruma, etc. The temple is run by friendly people who undoubtedly will offer you a cup of tea. Search about to find the resting place of Kyoto's late Daruma-painting artist, Steve Mindel.

ACCESS: A three-minute walk north from the junction of Marutamachi and Nishioji-dori, then right down a small side street. Marked with signposts. Bus nos. 202, 203, 204, and others.

Best Day Trip from Osaka

Nanko Yacho Koen, Osaka
Osaka-shi, Suminoe-ku, Nanko Kita 3-chome, 5-30.
Tel. (06) 613-5556. 9:00 A.M.–5:00 P.M. Closed Wednesdays.

You'll find sanctuary for humans, too, at the Nanko Yacho Koen, the wild bird sanctuary built on reclaimed land in the otherwise gloomy industrial wasteland at the end of the New Tram line. This is a forgotten "attraction" and that is what makes it all so attractive, especially at mid-week when the area is almost deserted. Near the entrance to Intex, the International Exhibition center, you can borrow a bicycle free of charge to take you to the sanctuary. At the heart of the park is a pavilion where waterfowl and seabirds intermingle around saline and freshwater ponds. Admission to the sanctuary and pavilion is free. Birds are identified in English and Japanese.

ACCESS: Yotsubashi Line subway to Suminoe Koen station, then New Tram Line to Nakafuto terminal, then a 1.6-kilometer cycle or leisurely stroll.

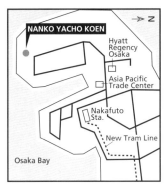

BEST EARLY MORNING MEDITATION

Ryozen-an, Kyoto
Kyoto-shi, Kita-ku, Murasakino, Daitokuji-cho 107. Tel. (075) 491-0543. Appointment required.

"I'm a skinhead but I'm not dangerous," quips Taiun Matsunami Roshi, the master of Daitoku-ji's Ryozen-an temple, as he introduces the basics of zazen meditation to a group of bleary-eyed but eager foreign students. Matsunami, who lectures on Zen in Europe every year, leads a small group of meditators every Wednesday through Sunday from 7:00 to 8:00 A.M. in this tranquil *zendo* (Zen study hall) in north Kyoto. Call ahead for booking. First time visitors are asked to arrive by 6:40 A.M. for an introductory talk. There is no charge, but a small donation is appreciated. Wear loose-fitting clothes and prepare for plenty of knee pain. You have to be able to sit in the lotus or semi-lotus position for the whole session.

ACCESS: Bus no. 204 to Daitokuji-mae bus stop. Ryozen-an is to the rear of the temple complex, just south of Imamiya-dori and Imamiya Jinja shrine.

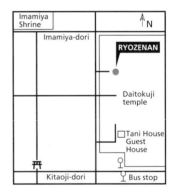

BEST EDO-PERIOD EROTICA

Edo Fuzoku Hihokan, Kyoto
Kyoto-shi, Ukyo-ku, Kiyotaki-mura, Kiyotaki Kanko Center. Tel. (075) 861-0243.

Perhaps "Best Social History Lesson" might be a more accurate, if less sensational, description of Kyoto's Edo Fuzoku Hihokan. Located beside the beautiful Kiyotaki Gorge, west of Kyoto, the Edo Fuzoku Hihokan is a collection of historical memorabilia and trivia assembled by the late Raizo Matsui, a remarkable gentleman whose life's work this tiny museum represents. At the heart of the collection is a veritable library of late Edo and early Meiji erotic literature, most notably, dozens of *makurabon* or "pillow books" that mothers once gave their daughters in preparation for their wedding night, and *shunga*, the erotic version of *ukiyo-e* woodblock prints. None other than the great Hokusai himself was wont to turn out *shunga* by the cartload, occasionally signing them "Shishoku Ganko," an allusion to a rampant male organ. At the Edo Fuzoku Hihokan, images of male and female genitalia—rampant or otherwise—abound, whether they be carved in wood, hidden on the underside of otherwise respectable statuettes, or inscribed on the back of a Buddha's rice-spatula (we are not making this up). Yet for all the willies and wotsits on display, the overall effect is one of edification rather than titillation. The late owner's daughter describes in detail the social mores of pre-industrial Japan, which took male chauvinism to unprecedented heights. We were surprised to learn that twin daughters were regularly abandoned, and that a pregnancy resulting in a baby girl was termed *chikushobara,* animal-stomach, or *inubara,* dog-stomach. On display is an original contract of a daughter sale. Just occasionally, the women got their revenge. Also on display is the front page of the *Osaka Shimbun* newspaper with the story of Abe Sada, a woman found wandering the streets of Tokyo in the 1930s with her lover's dismembered penis in her shopping bag. This story is told in the brilliant, but still banned film, *In the Realm of the Senses.* The Osaka tabloid features a graphic illustration that had our knees firmly clamped together. For all the sex and nudity, there's nothing prurient or sordid about the Edo Fuzoku Hihokan. You could bring your grandmother here. Admission free, but by appointment only.

ACCESS: In Kiyotaki village beside the Matsui's restaurant. Bus no. 62 from Sanjo Keihan station and bus no. 72 from Kyoto station leave for Kiyotaki hourly, and the journey takes approximately 50 minutes. Alternatively, take a taxi from Arashiyama Hankyu station, approximately a 15-minute ride.

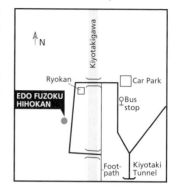

Best Fashion Museum

Kobe Fashion Bijutsukan, Kobe
Kobe-shi, Higashi Nada-ku, Koyo-machi 2-9.
Tel. (078) 858-0050.
Resource Center
Tel. (078) 858-0053. 11:00 A.M.–6:00 P.M. Fri. 11:00 A.M.– 8:00 P.M. Closed Wednesdays.

Rokko Island's temple to the art of body decoration and all that is excessive and gaudy is a must-see. Even the most stylistically challenged anorak-wearers will find something to fascinate in this gigantic fashion-victim's paradise. Looking like the mother ship from an early George Lucas movie, the museum is, however, far more than a humongous walk-in closet. The Resource Center on the third floor is a fantastic research base for anyone interested in the serious business of studying fashion, with thousands of magazines from around the world, CD-ROMs, movies, and old books; the photographs on display in the first floor Fashion Square feature originals from the likes of Helmut Newton, Nick Knight, and Irving Penn; and the UFO-inspired fifth floor dome holds a 424-seat concert hall. But the real stars of the Kobe Fashion Museum are the clothes themselves, from 17th-century European court dresses and Laotian tribal dresses to high couture 20th-century evening dresses. Make sure you have lots of time for browsing—and don't forget to leave your anorak at home. Admission: ¥500 for adults, ¥250 for school students and seniors over age 65.

ACCESS: Take the Rokko Liner monorail from either JR Sumiyoshi or Uozaki stations to the Island Center station. The museum is southeast of the station, alongside the Rokko Island Hospital.

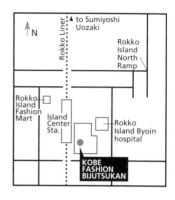

BEST FIRST DATE

Hankyu Koku Night Sky Walk, Osaka Prefecture
Yao-shi, Yao Kuko 2-12, Hankyu Kokunai.
Tel. (06) 943-0333. September to March only.

Twelve Minutes over Osaka. No, not the title of a B-movie, but the amount of time you and the object of your affections get zipping around the Osaka night sky for your ¥20,000. That's just enough time for the Cessna two-seater to fly over the Sky Building in Umeda and Osaka Harbor before you're whisked back to Yao Airport. A cool first date, but bring your own champagne. If you're really out to impress, why not rent a helicopter? (Twelve minutes for ¥70,000.)

ACCESS: A five-minute taxi ride from Yao Minami station on the Tanimachi subway line.

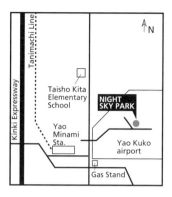

BEST GEISHA WATCHING

Kyoto-shi, Shinbashi, Gion, and Pontocho districts. Dusk.

As twilight approaches, the young kimono-clad apprentice geisha, known as *maiko,* head for their early evening rendezvous in the expensive traditional restaurants of Kyoto's Gion district. Their teachers, the fully fledged geisha (or *geiko,* as they are more properly known) are seldom seen, as they're more likely to be whisked to an appointment in the back of a Mercedes limo. These anachronistic figures of beauty, with their white-powdered faces and exquisitely painted necks are a link with time past, seemingly as fragile and as tough as the floating world they inhabit.

ACCESS: Shinbashi is in Gion, to the north and east of the intersection of Shijo-dori and Kawabata-dori. Pontocho is the first narrow paved street west of the Kamogawa river that runs north from Shijo. Keihan Shijo or Hankyu Kawaramachi stations. Well marked with signposts.

Best Giants Gas Station

Tanta Sekiyu, Kyoto
Kyoto-shi, Kita-ku, Murasakino, Nishino 60.
Tel. (075) 441-0940. 6:30 A.M.–midnight. Open every day.

"Nakashima is Baseball, Gasoline is Tanta!" proclaims the huge banner spread across the front of this north Kyoto gas stand. The owner is such a die-hard Yomiuri Giants fan that he cuts prices on the day following a Giants' win. Given their incredible form almost every season, this policy must cost him a small fortune. Expect at least a free lube inspection when they win the pennant. The part-time staff pledge allegiance to the Tokyo club (but we know for sure that at least one of them is a Yakult Swallows fan).

ACCESS: In front of Funaoka Park on the south side of Kitaoji-dori, between Senbon-dori and Horikawa-dori.

Best Glitz Palace

Hotel California, Osaka
Osaka-shi, Chuo-ku, Nishi-Shinsaibashi 1-9-30. Tel. (06) 943-0333. Open every day.

Shinsaibashi's temple to all that is American, or rather, all that a Japanese architect once imagined is American: Hotel California. This is a kitsch-lover's dream, and a reasonably priced place to stay in the heart of Osaka's Amerika-mura. Gilt staircases, wall-length mirrors, stuffed parrots, and livid-green plastic abound. The ground floor California Garden Bar resembles a Florida hairdressing salon from the early fifties. Single ¥7,000 per night; double ¥11,000. Check in any time you like (after 3:00 P.M.), but you may never leave . . .

ACCESS: Subway to Shinsaibashi station, Exit 8. Look for the palm trees painted atop an otherwise non-descript gray building.

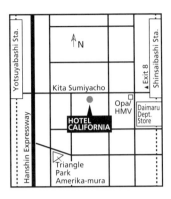

BEST HIDDEN TEMPLE

Iwaya Fudo (Iwayayama Shimyo-in), Kyoto
Kyoto-shi, Kita-ku, Kumogahata.
Tel. (075) 406-2061.

For all the vaunted beauty of Kyoto's famed places of worship, this tiny haven of Mikkyo (esoteric Buddhism) tucked away in the pine forests of Kumogahata is without question our favorite. Iwayayama Shimyo-in temple is a special place, both palpably spiritual and not a little spooky. The determinedly inaccessible location keeps away the tour buses that descend locust-like on Ginkakuji and Kiyomizu-dera temples. Thus Shimyo-in is a place for quiet reflection, a tranquil escape in the summer from the heat and the hassle of downtown Kyoto. Yet the temple seems to change moods. At times, the sunlight slanting down through the forest illuminates the *inari* fox gods, giving the place an air of gentle frivolity; at other times, the birds stop singing, the air feels colder, and only the brave venture up to the cave to offer prayers before the stern figure of the Dragon King.

The *fudo* Deva-King sculptures date back to A.D. 650. Shimyo-in is famed for its wild rhododendrons and magical healing water, but we just loved its mountain setting and almost animist simplicity.

On April 29, there is a fire-walking festival, performed by *yamabushi* mountain ascetics. Bring asbestos socks. Admission: ¥200. No photography allowed. If money is not a problem, stay overnight at the sole *ryokan* inn in these parts, **Rakuunso** (Tel. 075-406-2204). Otherwise, bring lunch. Great hiking in the surrounding hills.

ACCESS: by Bus no. 37 from Demachiyanagi Keihan station to Iwayabashi bus stop, then a brisk 1.2-kilometer uphill walk to the temple. Only three buses a day. The journey takes about 40 minutes, more if the narrow road is crowded.

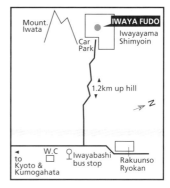

BEST HOT SPRING HIDEAWAY

Mugenkyo Onsen, Kyoto Prefecture

Kyoto-fu, Soraku-gun, Minami-Yamashiro, Tayama 38. Tel. (07439) 30515.

Seclusion, silence, and old-world charm are the chief attractions of Mugenkyo Onsen and the Tsurunoya Ryokan, an early Showa-era wooden inn which remains much the same as when it was built in 1929. Surrounded by thick forest, this is a perfect weekend getaway. Don't let the address fool you, it's more accessible from Nara than Kyoto. The carp cuisine is recommended.

ACCESS: Kansai Line to Tsukigase-guchi, from Kizu (Katamachi and Nara lines). Tsurunoya is a ten-minute taxi ride from the station.

BEST HOT WATER—OUTDOOR

Outdoor Resort Spa Horokuyu, Kyoto (Kurama Onsen)
Kyoto-shi, Sakyo-ku, Kurama Honmachi 520.
Tel. (075) 741-2131. Fax (075) 741-2375. Open-air bath,
10:00 A.M.–9:00 P.M. Open every day.

When all that temple-gazing or downtown shopping gets to be too much, head for the cool, leafy mountain village of Kurama and the delights of Kurama Onsen, a rural hot-spring haven just a 30-minute train ride from central Kyoto. "Healthy Resort Kurama Spa Horokuyu" has a variety of baths and food dishes on offer. We recommend a soak in the open-air *rotenburo* bath. This is where the master samurai Yoshitsune learned his swordsmanship from the long-nosed *tengu* goblins. We prefer to laze away in the waters. Open-air bath: ¥1,000. Bring your own towel. The spa can get awfully crowded on weekends, especially during the maple-viewing season, but mid-week it's blissfully quiet.

ACCESS: Eizan Dentetsu line from Keihan Demachiyanagi to Kurama station. Free shuttle bus or a brisk ten-minute walk.

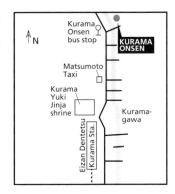

BEST INTERNATIONAL TOILETS

Osaka Business Park
Osaka-shi, Chuo-ku, Shiromi 1-3-7.
10:00 A.M.–6:00 P.M. Open every day.

Perform your most natural of functions in a variety of languages. The International Market Place, in Osaka Business Park, is a department store given over to pricey imported goods, but its most unique feature is undoubtedly "Toilets of the World." Each of the model lavatories contains fixtures and fittings imported from a different country. If you fancy something quick and clinical, we recommend the German. Those seeking something more flamboyant should head for the Italian.

ACCESS: Osaka Business Park exit from Keihan Kyobashi station. Clearly signposted.

BEST MAP OF KYOTO AND NARA

From the TIC, Kyoto
Kyoto-shi, Shimogyo-ku, Karasuma Shichijo Sagaru, Kyoto Tower Bldg., 1F.
Tel. (075) 371-5649. Mon.–Fri. 9:00 A.M.–5:00 P.M., Sat. 9:00 A.M.–noon.

The best map of Kyoto to be had is the one available from the TIC in Kyoto. It used to be free, but now costs ¥200. It's worth it, as it also lists tourist attractions and major bus routes throughout Kyoto. Longtime residents measure their stay by how many of these indispensable maps they've gone through. (For more information, see Best Advice—Tourist.)

ACCESS: Subway, JR, or Kintetsu lines to Kyoto station. On Karasuma-dori, ten meters north from Shionokoji-dori, directly beneath Kyoto Tower.

Best Nerd Watching

Denden Town, Osaka
Osaka-shi, Nihonbashi, Denden Town.

A surreal experience not for the faint of heart. This discount shopping area in Osaka's Nihonbashi is where the legions of computer and electronics nerds (known as *otaku*) come to feast their eyes on rows of cut-price electric goods. Mostly male, bespectacled, and feverish, they enthuse passionately about gigabytes, and exchange stories of hard drives and virtual love. Most frightening of all are the *otaku* couples, dressed in matching polo-neck sweaters, both clutching cardboard boxes full of the latest computer-game software. We think half of them are female, but it's hard to tell. Genuinely scary!

ACCESS: Tanimachi Line subway to Ebisucho station, exit 1A.

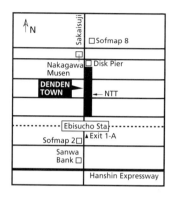

Best Peace Museum

Museum for World Peace, Kyoto
Kyoto-shi, Kita-ku, Tojiin Kitamachi 56-1.
Tel. (075) 465-8151. 9:30 A.M.–4:30 P.M. Closed Mondays, days following holidays, a week in August, and Dec. 28–Jan. 6.

Kansai actually boasts two peace museums, both excellent, but our vote goes to Ritsumeikan University's Kyoto Museum for World Peace, for its superlative, objective coverage of the Pacific War—including an honest account of Japan's political motives in invading Okinawa—and its global outlook, perhaps best exemplified by the one brilliant World Press Photo exhibition it hosts every year.

ACCESS: Bus nos. 15, 50, 52, or 55 to Ritsumeikan University. The museum is on Badai-dori, just southeast of the Ritsumeikan Daigaku bus stop.

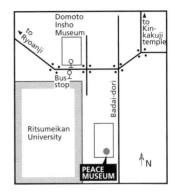

Best Photography

Prinz, Kyoto
Kyoto-shi, Sakyo-ku, Tanaka Takahara-cho 5.
Tel. (075) 712-3900. 11:00 A.M.–7:00 P.M. Closed Mondays.

This small gallery has excellent shows, including works by internationally renowned photographers such as Jan Saudek, Mary Ellen Mark, and Holly Warburton, as well as lesser-known artists. Prinz also has a postcard gallery and photography bookstore. Admission is free.

ACCESS: On Higashi Kuramaguchi-dori. Bus no. 204 to Tanaka Takahara-cho bus stop, or a three-minute walk from the Eizan Tetsudo railway Chayama station.

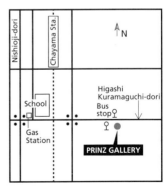

BEST RAINY DAY OUT

Panasonic Square, Osaka
Osaka-shi, Chuo-ku, Shiromi 2-1-61, Twin 21 National Tower, 2F.
Tel. (06) 949-2122. 10:00 A.M.–6:00 P.M. Open every day.

Have a computerized tarot reading or your visage beautifully inscribed on a *hanko* personal seal (¥1,000), via a camera-computer interface courtesy of the technical wizards of National Panasonic in the Yume Shashinkan (Dream-Photo Studio). Similar technology allows couples to predict what their future offspring will look like. Our gay friends had lots of fun with this one. Or else get your picture inscribed on the face of a proboscis monkey, so all your friends can say "Ha! No difference!" Free video games, but avoid weekends or school holidays when the competition to play Street Fighter 2 is more violent than the action on the screen. Lots of fun. Admission: ¥500.

ACCESS: A five-minute walk from Kyobashi station on the Keihan and Tsurumi lines subway in the Twin 21 building.

BEST SECLUDED GARDEN

Kikokutei, Kyoto
Kyoto-shi, Shimogyo-ku, Shimojuzuya-dori, Higashi Hongan-ji
Tel. (075) 371-2961. Open 9:00 A.M.–4:00 P.M. Open every day.

An oasis of tranquility in the heart of Kyoto. Experts will recognize this as a fine example of a Fujiwara-period garden, but we just love the lake, the silence, and the absence of other visitors. And it is no longer necessary to apply in advance for a visit to Higashi Hongan-ji temple. Watch out for the bees. Free admission.

ACCESS: A five-minute walk from Kyoto JR or Keihan Shichijo stations. One block northwest of the junction of Shichijo-dori and Kawaramachi-dori.

BEST SLEEP

Tawaraya Ryokan, Kyoto
Kyoto-shi, Nakagyo-ku, Fuyacho-dori, Anekoji Agaru.
Tel. (075) 211-5566. Check in: noon; check out: 11:00 A.M.
Some credit cards accepted. English spoken.

If not the best sleep, this is at least the most expensive. The favored Kyoto refuge for foreign luminaries, rock stars, and politicians. Past guests have included Mikhail Gorbachev, Marlon Brando, and the Rothschilds. You, too, can rub shoulders with the superstars at this most quintessential of Kyoto *ryokan,* but you'll have to book up to a year in advance. We couldn't sleep for worrying about the bill. From ¥35,000 to ¥75,000 per person, excluding service charges and tax.

ACCESS: On Fuyacho-dori just south of Oike-dori, a five-minute walk from Oike subway station.

BEST TOURIST TEMPLE

Sanzen-in, Kyoto
Kyoto-shi, Sakyo-ku, Ohara, Raigei-in 540.
Tel. (075) 744-2531. 8:30 A.M.–4:30 P.M. Open every day.

Forget the downtown frills and flashiness of pavilions gold and silver, and head for the leafy quiet of Ohara and the wonderful Tendai sect's Sanzen-in temple, which exudes artistry from every pore. Unless it's maple-viewing season, that is, when the temple resembles the Osaka loop line at rush hour. But even then it's marvelous.

SIGHTS 79

ACCESS: Take the Kyoto bus from Keihan Demachiyanagi station bound for Yase Ohara as far as the Ohara bus stop, then follow the signs up the hill. About 30 minutes.

BEST YAKUZA WATCHING

Gojo and Shichijo districts, Kyoto
Kyoto-shi, Shimogyoku, Gojo/Shichijo.

As heart-stopping adventure sports go, *yakuza*-watching has to be on a par with bungee jumping and lion-taming, but the casual gangster-spotter is on fairly safe ground strolling the back streets between Kyoto's Gojo and Shichijo streets, headquarters of the gang group Aizu Kotetsu. A particularly rich hunting ground is the narrow street running north-south one block east of the Japanese Inn Group's **Hiraiwa Ryokan** (Tel. 075-371-2709), a popular, and despite the location, safe budget hotel just a ten-minute walk from Kyoto station. Look for swarthy gentlemen with "punch perms," black limousines, and a deficit of fingers. The local bathhouse, Ume-yu, is the place for the adventurous to check out authentic Japanese gang tattoos. Incidentally, the imposing Meiji-era building on Shomen-dori, next door to the Aizu Kotetsu head office, is the original headquarters of Nintendo. Though the *yakuza* largely keep to themselves, visitors should be wary. One night we walked through this area and suddenly the street was filled with scores of policemen in bullet-proof vests. You might like to bring yours.

ACCESS: A ten-minute walk north-east from Kyoto station, north of Shomen-dori.

Bars

BEST BOURBON WITH A BITE

O Bar Osaka, Osaka
Osaka-shi, Chuo-ku, Minami-Senba 4-4-8, Creative Shinsaibashi, 7F.
Tel. (06) 245-2666. 7:00 P.M.–3:00 A.M., Fri., Sat. 7:00 P.M.–5:00 A.M. Open every day.

Where else but in Japan could you find a downtown bar atop a seven-story office building that boasts as its main attraction two black-tipped reef sharks? At O Bar Osaka yuppie-ish customers wind down after a hard day at the office, lulled into a trance-like state of relaxation by the hypnotic twists and turns of the resident, ever-circling, giant celapods. Or perhaps it has something to do with the sixty varieties of bourbon on offer. This is a fun place for a date, but it's the last place we want to be when the big earthquake strikes. ¥500 table charge. Drinks from ¥600.

ACCESS: On the northwest corner of the junction of Midosuji and Nagahori-dori, directly opposite the Cosmo Service Station. Midosuji Line subway to Shinsaibashi station, exit 3.

BEST CANDLELIT NIGHTCAP

Mekhong, Kyoto
Kyoto-shi, Kita-ku, Nishigamo Mizugaki-cho 79.
Tel. (075) 495-9292. 6:00 P.M.–2:00 A.M. Closed Mondays.
English spoken. No credit cards.

Had Boris Karloff had a penchant for Thai rum and excellent, inexpensive Japanese food, this north Kyoto restaurant is where he'd have hung out. Mekhong is part student haunt, part date spot, and part late-night bar, dominated by huge gothic wax candles which slowly melt into fantastic shapes as you watch. The flickering candlelight gradually hypnotizes you into ordering yet another of those wonderful fruity cocktails. The room may be dark, but the atmosphere is anything but, with friendly staff and a relaxed, largely student clientele. Mekhong is slightly off the beaten track, but this doesn't seem to deter customers—it's always full. Hardly a surprise, for the food is uniformly excellent, though portions are slightly on the small side. We had double helpings of the *ebi to mentaiko no harumaki,* tiny spring rolls with spicy cod-roe and shrimp (¥650). Irresistible. Also recommended are *kinoko no garikku itame*, stir-fried mushrooms with garlic (¥600); Mekhong Salad, which has tofu, baby tomatoes, and boiled egg covered with a tasty peanut dressing (¥800); and *jako mentaiko gohan*, spicy cod-roe with whitefish on rice (¥400). Singha beer (¥650) and Ebisu beer (¥500) complement the food, but where Mekhong really excels is in the cocktails made with the Thai rum that gives this place its name. We loved the sinfully easy-to-drink Nha Trang, made with pineapple juice, papaya, and rum (¥700), and stayed way too long drinking these smooth, seductive confections while chatting with owner-traveler Suzuki-san. It was so relaxing we felt for a while we were back on Ko Pi Pi.

ACCESS: A minute's walk southeast of Nishigamo Shako bus terminal in north Kyoto, opposite K-mart. The buses stop early. When they do, access is by taxi from Kitaoji bus terminal, about a ten-minute ride.

Best Classic Stand-up Boozer

Kimura Sakaten, Kyoto
Kyoto-shi, Kamigyo-ku, Demachi-dori Masugata Agaru. Tel. (075) 231-1341. Early morning until 7:30 P.M. Irregular holidays. No credit cards.

From the outside, this *tachinomi* ("stand-up bar") in Kyoto's Demachiyanagi district, is unprepossessing, without even a sign to announce its name. Yet this is an astonishing place, full of some of the oddest and most remarkable characters that this inveterate bar-crawler has ever met. Laborers, artists, businessmen, down-and-outs, and all manner of weird and wonderful customers squeeze into this tiny space to talk politics, drink, squabble, and inevitably drink more. At times you feel as if you've walked onto the set of *Blade Runner*. All this is presided over by a diminutive and very sprightly grandmother, who we take to be Kimura-san herself. When we inquired how long the shop had existed, she blithely answered, "Four hundred years and twelve generations." Indeed, the place reeks not only of spilled beer and stale tobacco, but of historical foment and clandestine meetings.

Beer and saké are sold at vending-machine prices. The law forbids *tachinomi* bars to sell cooked food, so try some dried squid, fish sausage, or a triangle of processed cheese from the ancient candy jars that line the walls. Tell Kimura-san what you want, and she'll write your bill on the tabletop in chalk. Expect to receive a lot of attention here from the oft-inebriated locals. This is beer-and-sawdust, not wine-and-cheese, and we imagine it can sometimes get quite rough and ready (perhaps this is why no women customers are allowed). About as un-typical a Kyoto experience as you can get.

ACCESS: On Kawaramachi-dori, 100 meters north of Imadegawa. From Demachiyanagi station on the Keihan line head west across Demachiyanagi Bridge at the confluence of the two rivers, and turn right up Kawaramachi. A three-minute walk.

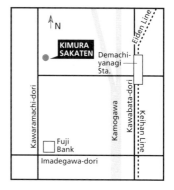

BEST COZY LATE-NIGHT COCKTAILS

Matera, Osaka
Osaka-shi, Chuo-ku, Higashi-Shinsaibashi 2-8-21, Nippo Tatamiyamachi Kaikan, 3F.
Tel./Fax (06) 211-7855. 8:00 P.M.–5:00 A.M. Occasionally closed Sundays. English spoken. No credit cards.

There's no matte black in sight at this eight-seater bar, and you'll always receive a warm welcome from master Kenta Kobayashi, who serves up cocktails with a flourish that reminds us of the time he spent in Sicily, as does the three-legged tattoo on his upper left arm. Matera wakes up when Shinsaibashi is winding down, with the hostesses and patrons coming in for some non-business fun around 3:00 A.M., but it's good to go here anytime for a relaxing drink. Cocktails from ¥500.

88 THE BEST OF KANSAI

ACCESS: A five-minute walk from Shinsaibashi subway station, around the corner from the Shinsaibashi branch of Pig and Whistle, on the east side of Tatamiyamachi-suji. It's the third building in from Suomachi-suji, opposite the Awaji Wine Bar.

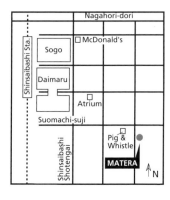

BEST METALHEAD BAR

Jam House, Kyoto
Kyoto-shi, Shimogyo-ku, Kiyamachi Shijo Sagaru.
Tel. (075) 351-8202. Weekdays, Sun. 5:00 P.M.–3:00 A.M.
Sat. 7:00 P.M.–5:00 A.M. English spoken. No credit cards.

Jam House was Kyoto's first ever *rokku kissa,* the kind of coffee shop devoted to the sinful vice of rock 'n' roll that sprang up throughout Japan in the late sixties. Today it's a hangout for Kyoto's many amateur bands, who usually come here for post-gig partying. Spandex leotards, leather boots, and fishnet stockings are *de rigeur,* and that's only the men. You may be, er, lucky enough to run into the crimson-haired, heavily tattooed, female vocalist of local heroes Sperma, or perhaps the lead singer of the equally popular Zenryoku Onanies (the Full-Force Masturbators), an amiable fellow given to wrapping himself in saran wrap both on and off stage. Quench your thirst with an Axl Rose Cocktail, "for bad boys and girls only," and request your favorite record from the thousand or so on offer. See if you can get Kichi, the owner, to show you his photo collection. Lots of fun, and cheap for a late-night downtown beer.

ACCESS: A five-minute walk south of Hankyu Line Kawaramachi station, on Kiyamachi-dori, about 100 meters from the Pink Tomato massage club.

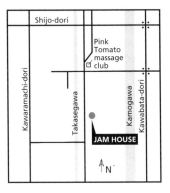

BEST MICROBREWERY

Kotobuki Shuzo, Osaka Prefecture
Osaka-fu, Takatsuki-shi, Tomita-machi 3-26-12.
Tel. (0726) 96-0003. 8:30 A.M.–10:00 P.M. (Last beer-tasting session begins at 6:00 P.M.). Open every day.

With the onset of each new season, Japan's beer-making conglomerates bombard we hapless consumers with dozens of "new" beers, most of which are completely identical. Kirin's Autumn Dream competes with Asahi's Autumn Sonata which challenges Suntory's Autumn Wonder and so on, ad nauseam, all in the name of refreshment and mega-yen profits. Respite from the tide of dishwater comes courtesy of Takatsuki's saké-maker turned micro-brewer, Kotobuki Shuzo. Their Osaka Kuninocho Beer, styled as a German-type draft, reminds us more of a British light brown ale with added kick, but whatever you call it, we like its flavorful, deep taste. Not cheap at ¥600 for a 330-milliliter bottle, but it is a delightful change from mass-produced soapsuds. Available only in selected liquor stores. Groups of 10 to 20 people are welcome to tour the brewery and sample the product from the source, at ¥2,000 per person. Bring your own snacks, or the brewery can provide hors d'oeuvres for an additional ¥1,000.

ACCESS: Less than a ten-minute walk from Hankyu Tonda station. Turn right out of the station, head west and turn left in front of the train crossing. Turn left again at the Maruyoshi Beikokuten rice shop, and Kotobuki Shuzo is on the left.

BEST-NAMED BAR

Post Coitus, Kyoto
Kyoto-shi, Sakyo-ku, Tanaka, Asukai-cho 45-2.
Tel. (075) 781-4152. 7:00 P.M.–2:00 A.M. Closed Sundays.
No credit cards.

A spooky place with bare white walls, a Vincent Price candelabra, and a total absence of humor, this cocktail bar is heavy on the froid and short on the sang. Trendy, cool to the point of refrigeration, but we love the Cuba Libres almost as much as the nomenclature. Was it good for you? Honorable mention in this category goes to Osaka's Soul Fucktry.

ACCESS: About 100 meters north from the junction of Imadegawa and Higashioji-dori, down a small side street to the right. Look for the Fujii paint shop on the corner.

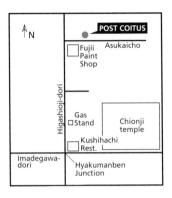

Best Reggae Cave Izakaya

Rasta King, Kyoto
Kyoto-shi, Nakagyo-ku, Kiyamachi, Sanjo Sagaru Yamazaki-cho 245, Clairon Bldg., 5F.
Tel. (075) 256-4567. 6:00 P.M.–5:00 A.M. (Last food order at 3:00 A.M.) Open every day. English spoken. No credit cards.

Every once in a while we are seized with the uncontrollable desire to eat charcoal-grilled chicken *yakitori* in a dimly lit pagan cave-dwelling, surrounded by groups of partying youths and images of strange heathen deities, whereupon we head immediately for Rasta King, an *izakaya*-cum-reggae bar which doubles as a kind of troglodyte loft in the heart of Kyoto's Kiyamachi. Customers squat at low tables in stygian darkness, feasting on traditional Japanese *izakaya* cuisine, including *hokke* mackerel and *shishamo* sardines grilled over hot coals in ceramic hibachi grills (¥500). We could have called this Best Place Not to Read *War and Peace*. Fun.

ACCESS: A five-minute walk south of Sanjo-dori on the east side of the Takase River. Nearest station: Keihan Sanjo. Down the small street immediately north of the Bal Building on Kawaramachi-dori, on the fifth floor of the first large building to your left. Look for the Rasta flag.

Best Shutterbug Bar

Hachimonjiya, Kyoto
Kyoto-shi, Nakagyo-ku, Kiyamachi-dori, Shijo Agaru, Onishi Bldg., 3F.
Tel. (075) 256-1731. Early evening until early morning. Open every day. No credit cards.

Photographer Kai Fusayoshi's Kiyamachi hostelry is a hangout for a weird and wonderful assortment of oddballs, artists, intellectual types, drunks, and—of course—photographers in downtown Kyoto. Customers congregate at the counter bar, or cluster around the few tables, all of which are piled high with art and photography books. This is the sort of venue where it is natural to discuss the most recent work by Nobuyoshi Araki, or the latest political rumblings from Kyoto University's leftists. Dark to the point of dinginess, this is the place to nurse a beer and pontificate upon whatever takes your fancy. You might meet someone famous.

ACCESS: On Kiyamachi-dori, a five-minute walk north from Shijo. Look for the public-phone booth bedecked with pictures of naked women; Hachimonjiya is on the third floor of the building beside it.

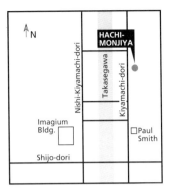

Entertainment

BEST AAAARGH!

Fureai Sports Daigo, Kyoto
Kyoto-shi, Fushimi-ku, Momoyama-cho, Yamanoshita 19-6. Tel. (075) 603-0410. 10:00 A.M.–6:00 P.M. Open every day.

Suicidal thrill-seekers need travel no farther than the Kyoto suburb of Daigo for their elasticated masochism. Jaded bungee lovers may wish to opt for the reverse *gyaku-banjii* where willing victims are strapped to a chair tethered by two pieces of industrial-strength rubber stretched between two towers. The chair is fixed to terra firma until you give the command, at which point you are rocketed skyward. Throw up and your lunch will reach Osaka. Regular bungee: ¥2,000. *Gyaku banjii:* ¥2,000 per person for two, ¥2,800 for lone loonies.

ACCESS: Keihan Line to Rokujizo station, then a seven-minute walk. Listen for the screams.

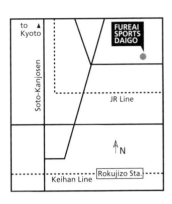

Best Cinema

Minami Kaikan, Kyoto
Kyoto-shi, Minami-ku, Nishi-Kujo Higashi Hieijo-cho 78. Tel. (075) 661-3993. 9:45 A.M.–10:30 P.M. Open every day. Closed January 1.

A general-release cinema that also shows art-house circuit and non-mainstream films. This was the first Kansai movie house to discover Quentin Tarantino, Mike Leigh, etc. The late show every day finishes at 10:30 P.M. A little off the beaten track, but the inspired selection of offerings makes this place worth seeking out. Admission ¥1,700.

ACCESS: 150 meters west of Toji station on the Kintetsu Line.

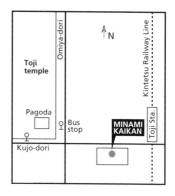

Best Discount Tickets

Kyoto Ticketshop, Kyoto
Kyoto-shi, Kamigyo-ku, Sasaya-machi Senbon Nishi, Sasaya-cho 4-304-7.
Tel. (075) 464-7746. 10:00 A.M.–7:00 P.M. Closed Sundays.

One is never quite sure about the legality of these cut-rate ticket operations, of which Kyoto Ticketshop is currently the best, but who really cares with savings of about ten percent on *shinkansen* (bullet train) tickets, phone cards, beer coupons, and all manner of prepaid cards? The real bargains are on the much-traveled Osaka–Tokyo and Osaka–Hakata *shinkansen* routes. Expect savings of about ¥1,600 on ordinary, and ¥3,700 on Green Car (first-class) one-way tickets. We like to buy Green Car deluxe tickets here, which cost roughly the same as a standard non-discounted ticket bought at a JR window. This small luxury is especially worth it during holiday season, when the regular cars are like sardine tins.

ACCESS: On Senbon-dori, two streets south of Imadegawa-dori. Bus nos. 50, 55, 201, or 203 to Senbon Imadegawa.

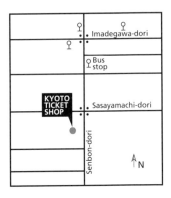

BEST ELVIS

Masaaki "Elvis" Takakura, Kyoto
Tel. 030-708-5256/(0774) 52-6150/Fax. (0774) 54-0307
Live House Nashville
Kyoto-shi, Nakagyo-ku, Onmae-dori, Shijo Sagaru.
Tel. (075) 311-6255. Reservations required.

Elvis lives! Not only that, but he lives in Kyoto, drives a beat-up Harley, and he's a plumber. Masaaki Takakura, Kansai's King of Rock 'n' Roll, is available for your wedding or birthday party, or you can catch him at Live House Nashville every Saturday night, when he joins forces with country band The Nashville Five. Takakura-san is at pains to point out that he's not an Elvis freak, but an Elvis *song* freak, thus he eschews sequined jumpsuits for jeans and a Harley T-shirt. Yet the 47-year-old sanitation engineer did christen his daughter Lisa Marie, and when he talks of the time he saw Elvis play in Las Vegas in 1971, his eyes glaze over and he almost whispers, "it was like a dream."

Takakura-san is a hoot, and is guaranteed to turn

even the most staid gathering into a roaring Elvisfest. Call well in advance, in Japanese, for reservations. Saturday night gigs at Live House Nashville have sets at 9:00, 10:00, and 11:00 P.M. No admission fee. No table charge.

ACCESS: Bus nos. 3, 203, or others to Shijo-Onmae bus stop. A two-minute walk south on Onmae-dori, or a five-minute walk east from Hankyu Sai-in station.

BEST FIRE FESTIVAL

Kurama Hi-Matsuri, Kyoto
Kyoto-shi, Sakyo-ku, Kurama Yuki Jinja.
Tel. (075) 741-2138. October 22. 6:00 P.M.–midnight.

Perhaps more of a pagan ritual than a sacred rite, with elements of a purification ceremony and a contest of strength thrown in, the Kurama Fire Festival is one of the region's most spectacular events. On the night of October 22, village strongmen congregate in Kurama to carry five-meter-long burning torches to the local shrine. Iron baskets filled with wood are enthusiastically burned outside each house. The climax comes late at night when the torch carriers meet on the steps of Kurama Yuki Shrine. Unmissable. Get there as early in the afternoon as you can with picnic snacks and a good book because after 4:00 P.M., access is nearly impossible.

ACCESS: Eizan Dentetsu Line from Kyoto Demachiyanagi to Kurama station. Special trains run into the night. Getting there and away is easiest by bicycle.

Best Free Movies

Japan Foundation, Kyoto
Kyoto-shi, Nakagyo-ku, Karasuma Nishiki Agaru, Yasuda Kasai Kaijo Bldg., 8F.
Tel. (075) 211-1312.

Every Wednesday the Japan Foundation's Kyoto branch shows free Japanese movies with English subtitles beginning at 2:00 P.M. Each month there is a different theme. Recent offerings have included samurai dramas and fantasy animation. Alas, this series is open to non-Japanese nationals only. While you are here, check out the 5,000-volume library of books on Japan. Most are in English.

ACCESS: In the Yasuda Kasai Kaijo building on the west side of Karasuma street, just north of Nishikikoji-dori. A three-minute walk from Karasuma Hankyu subway station.

BEST FRENCH MOVIES

Cinema Verite, Osaka
Osaka-shi, Kita-ku, Doyama-cho 5-9, Ogi Kaikan, B1. Tel. (06) 361-4310. 9:00 A.M.–10:30 P.M. Open every day.

This is the place to check out vintage Alain Delon films or the latest Parisian new-wave offerings with, miracle of miracles, subtitles in both English and Japanese.

ACCESS: Tanimachi subway line to Higashi-Umeda station. Walk toward Izumi no Hiroba, exit 6. Located in the basement below Izakaya Horai.

BEST GAY CINEMA

Cine Friends Nishijin, Kyoto
Kyoto-shi, Kamigyo-ku, Senbon-dori, Nishijin Kyogoku Higashi Iru.
Tel. (075) 441-1460. Noon–9:00 P.M. Fri. and Sat. noon–dawn.

Something of a Kyoto "underground" institution, Cine Friends Nishijin (slogan: "Meeting with Movies, Meeting with that Special Man") shows films from Japan and southeast Asia, with very occasional art movies by the likes of Derek Jarman. Yet the emphasis is on home-grown cinema for the *barazoku,* "rose people" or gay men. (Is that a ceremonial sword in your pocket, or are you just pleased to see me?) One recent movie featured gay sumo wrestlers! Straight thrill-seekers are confined to the first floor. The basement and second floor are a "play zone." Proceed with caution. Admission ¥1,500, ¥800 before 1:00 P.M.

ACCESS: A five-minute walk south of the junction of Senbon-dori and Imadegawa-dori, in the narrow alleyway known as Nishijin Kyogoku. Bus nos. 201, 55, or others.

BEST LIBRARY

Nichibunken, Kyoto
Kyoto-shi, Nishikyo-ku, Goryo, Oeyama 3-2.
Tel. (075) 335-2100. Mon.–Fri. 9:00 A.M.–5:00 P.M.

Perched preposterously at the top of a mountain outside Kyoto, in a palatial neo-Gothic mansion belonging to the Ministry of Education, the Kokusai Nihon Bunka Kenkyu Center Nichibunken (Center for Japanese Research) library is a treasure house of books on every conceivable aspect of Japan past and present, a Japanophile researcher's dream come true. Strictly speaking this library is reserved for Japanese university-affiliated users, but we've never been asked to provide ID. A serious demeanor and a mountain of papers clutched under one arm seems to do the trick. Try wearing a beret.

For those unwilling or unable to make the trek up the mountain, the Japan Foundation Library downtown comes an honorable, if very distant, second. (See Best Free Movies.)

ACCESS: Kyoto bus from the west exit of Hankyu Katsura station. Buses run once an hour at best. If traveling under your own steam, take Gojo-dori (Route 9) west until you reach Rakusai New Town (about 10 km), turn right at the clearly marked sign. It's a good 15-minute hike uphill.

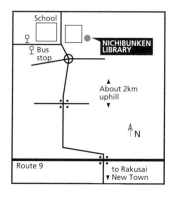

BEST LIVE HOUSE

Taku-Taku, Kyoto
Kyoto-shi, Shimogyo-ku, Tominokoji Bukkoji Sagaru. Tel. (075) 351-1321. 6:00 P.M.–9:00 P.M. Open every day. English spoken.

Mostly local bands play here, but just occasionally the likes of Dr. John, Otis Rush, Taj Mahal, and The Neville Brothers grace the stage at this small downtown Kyoto live house. So do the Cockney Cocks, Bad Smell, and our favorites, Gembaku Onanies (the "Atomic Masturbators"). With a maximum capacity of 200, you're close enough to the stage to get spat upon—or hear the golden voice of Aaron Neville. The average admission charge of ¥1,800 (depending on the headliner) includes one drink.

ACCESS: Exit 11 from Hankyu Kawaramachi station. Turn south down Tominokoji-dori. About a two-minute walk south of Shijo.

Best Oops Upside Your Head

Orochi, Osaka Prefecture
Suita-shi, Senri Banpaku Koen 1-1, Expoland.
Tel. (06) 877-0560. 9:30 A.M.–5:30 P.M. Open later during holidays. Closed Wednesdays, and days following holidays.

Kansai's most popular attraction, this "inverted coaster" gives the traditional rollercoaster a new twist, literally, as you are suspended by your shoulders with your feet dangling, speeding along at 90 kilometers per hour on the 1,200-meter track. Admission to Expoland ¥1,000, Orochi ¥800.

ACCESS: In Expoland, in front of Banpaku Kinen Koen station on the Osaka Monorail.

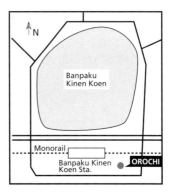

BEST PLACE TO SHOOT YOUR FRIENDS

Padou, Osaka
Osaka-shi, Nishi-ku, Chiyozaki 3-chome Kita 2.
Tel. (06) 583-5100. 10:00 A.M –11:30 P.M. Open every day.

The place to watch humble high school girls transform themselves into brutal, laser-toting maniacs. Q-Tag laser-shooting gallery is the showpiece of Sega Arena, the mother of all game centers, located in the Padou entertainment complex next to the 55,000-seat Osaka Dome. Participants don luminous life-jacket-like waistcoats, to which are attached murder weapons, and are divided into two opposing teams. When the bell rings, despite strict instructions not to run, all hell breaks loose, as people try to vaporize each other to smithereens. It's most fun, of course, to be on the opposite team as your friends.

The secret is not only to shoot as many opponents as possible, but also to avoid being shot yourself, as we found out to our own cost. When the bell rang to signal the end of the duel, we had more holes than an acupuncturist's dummy. Final rankings are given in English, a subtle inference that the best psychopaths come from abroad? Alas, we were more Norman Needlebaum than Arnold Schwarzenegger. At ¥600 for three minutes, Q-Tag is slightly more expensive second-for-second than a Tokyo-bound *shinkansen,* but it's worth it for the sheer pleasure of reducing your mates to piles of smoldering molecules.

ACCESS: A five-minute walk from Taisho station on the JR Kanjo-sen loop line. Turn right out of the station, cross Iwamatsu-bashi bridge and Padou is 100 meters on your left.

Best Reggae Warehouse

Jugglin' Rink City, Osaka Prefecture

Osaka-fu, Izumi-sano-shi, Rinku Orai Minami Rinku Park Nai. Tel. (0724) 69-0680. 7:00 P.M.–1:00 A.M. Fri., Sat., and days before holidays 7:00 P.M.–4:00 A.M. Open every day.

The hotsteppers of southern Osaka congregate at this giant reggae hall down in Izumi-sano. The reggae vibes are blasted out across the 1,800-square-meter dance floor by a wall of "Killasan" speakers, pumping out 50,000 watts of heavy dub stylee. Most of the customers are in their twenties, but even silver-dreadlocked *gaijin* are unlikely to stand out in this 1,000-person-plus hangar. Resident Jamaican DJ. Weekend admission: ¥2,000 (includes one drink). Mon.–Thurs.: ¥1,000.

ACCESS: A two-minute walk from JR and Nankai Rinku Town station. Last train, 11:00 P.M., first train, 5:45 A.M.

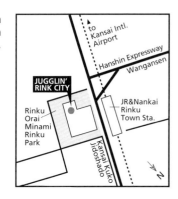

BEST STAND-UP-AND-DO-YOUR-THING

Kyoto Connection, Kyoto

Kyoto-shi, Kita-ku, Shichiku, Kurisu-cho, Asakura Bldg., 2F. Tel. (075) 712-7129 / (075) 561-7557. Last Sat. of the month (except August and December) from 8:30 P.M.

This place is for all of you eccentric, artistic types who feel the urge to get up and recite Icelandic poetry, sing the Hawaiian blues, or play the Jomon-period nose flute. Spend an eclectic evening full of music, poetry, performance, or whatever else organizers Ken Rodgers and Ken Burch have managed to drum up this month. The Kyoto Connection is a great place to meet people, hang out, or let it all hang out. A ¥500 donation is requested for charity.

ACCESS: City bus nos. 46 or 66 from Shijo Kawaramachi or Shijo Omiya. Get off at the Ushiwaka bus stop and walk north for one minute.

BEST TUNES

Diva, Osaka

Osaka-shi, Chuo-ku, Higashi-Shinsaibashi 1-17-15, Marusei Bldg., 6F.
Tel. (06) 241-9733. Mon.–Thurs. 7:00 P.M.–1:00 A.M. Fri. and Sat. 7:00 P.M.–3:00 A.M. Sun. and holidays 7:00 P.M.–midnight.

Embarrass your friends with your Ella Fitzgerald and Sid Vicious impersonations. Karaoke heaven, with more than 4,000 songs in English and 5,000 more from around Asia. ¥1,500 admission. Patrons are required to order at least one drink.

ACCESS: Midosuji Line to Shinsaibashi station, exit 6. Turn right down Shinsaibashi-suji then left for two blocks. On the left side of the street, just past the Atrium.

Best Video Rental

Video Station, Kyoto
Kyoto-shi, Sakyo-ku, Hyakumanben Kosaten Agaru, Hyakumangoku Bldg., 1F.
Tel. (075) 712-4050. 11:00 A.M.–3:00 A.M. Open every day.

Excellent collection of videos, from Laurel and Hardy to Luchino Visconti and Tom Hanks to Tarkovsky. Particularly strong on oddball or underground video, and lots of classic old Japanese movies with some English subtitles. Membership fee: ¥380. Sadly, membership is limited to people who live or work in Sakyo-ku, Kita-ku, Nakagyo-ku, Kamigyo-ku, or Higashiyama-ku.

ACCESS: A five-minute walk east from Keihan Demachiyanagi station, just north of the intersection of Imadegawa-dori and Higashioji-dori. Convenient from any of the many buses that go to Hyakumanben.

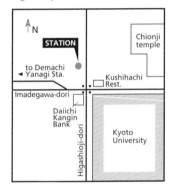

Best What's On

Kansai Time Out, Kobe
Kobe-shi, Chuo-ku, 1-13 Ikuta-cho 1-chome.
Tel. (078) 232-4516/7. Fax (078) 232-4518.
E-mail: ktoedit@kto.co.jp. Mon.–Fri. 10:00 A.M.–5:30 P.M.
Closed weekends.

Films. Festivals. Lonely Hearts. Sayonara Sales. Job Offers. All are to be found in *Kansai Time Out,* Kansai's indispensable monthly information magazine, which has survived earthquakes both literal and financial while serving the foreign community of western Japan for the last two decades. The recently introduced Ombudsman page is a particularly welcome addition. Available from major bookstores for ¥300 per issue, or by subscription (¥3,000 per year). Owner/publisher Dave Jack refuses to price the magazine above the cost of a cup of coffee, making *KTO* a genuine Kansai rarity—a bargain. (Downstairs is Wantage Books, whose profits support the Kansai Bangladesh Project.)

ACCESS: Down the small side street alongside the photo processing shop diagonally opposite the massive shopping complex OPA. A ten-minute walk uphill from Sannomiya, or two minutes from Shin-Kobe subway station.

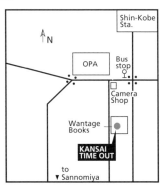

BEST WHIPS AND CHAINS

Barajujikan, Kyoto
Kyoto-shi, Nakagyo-ku, Takasegawa Kado, Shijo Agaru, Kiyamachi 367.
Tel. (075) 212-0277. 7:00 P.M.–1:00 A.M. Closed Sundays.

If your thing is to be tied up and chastized by a lady in high heels and a black rubber suit, Barajujikan can't (if you'll pardon the phrase) be beaten. For lovers of the lash, voyeurs, and other denizens of darkness, although the overall effect might be more Marx Brothers than Marquis de Sade. Show ticket: ¥6,000–¥10,000.

ACCESS: Two-minute walk northeast of the junction of Shijo-dori and Kawaramachi-dori.

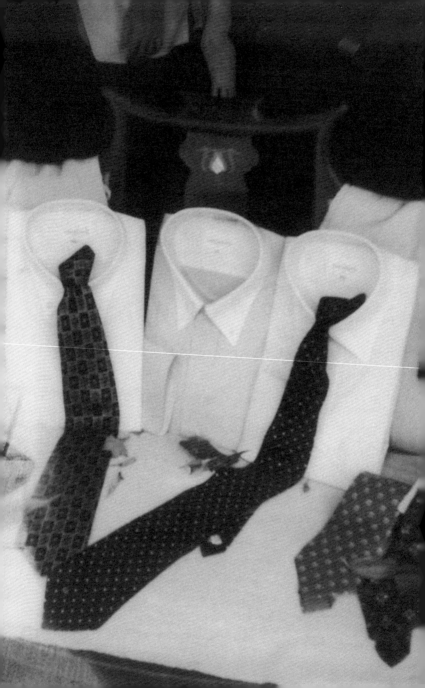

Shopping

BEST ANTIQUE STREET

Shinmonzen-Dori, Kyoto
Kyoto-shi, Higashiyama-ku, Shinmonzen-dori.
English is spoken at most of these stores.

M. Nakai. Lacquerware, *tansu* chests, and textiles.
   Tel. (075) 561-2906. 9:00 A.M.– 6:00 P.M. Closed Mondays.
Kaji's Antiques. Byobu painted screens.
   Tel. (075) 561-4114. 9:00 A.M.–6:00 P.M. Closed Mondays.
Tenpyodo. Wonderfully ornate Korean furniture.
   Tel. (075) 561-5688. 10:00 A.M.–6:00 P.M. Open every day.
Yamada Art Gallery. Modern prints—most notably, those of Shiko Munakata.
   Tel. (075) 561-5382. 10:00 A.M.– 6:00 P.M. Closed Mondays.
T. Ikegami and Takebi. Bronze, lacquerware.
   Tel. (075) 541-4563. 10:00 A.M.–6:00 P.M. Open every day.
Rakuyo Shoten. Ceramics, netsuke, and a whole treasure trove of "selected Asian objects."
   Tel. (075) 541-4825. 10:00 A.M.–6:00 P.M. Open every day.
R. Kita. Imari and Kutani ceramics ("Over 150 yers old [sic]," as they say), including our favorite, the gorgeous red Kutani.
   Tel. (075) 561-6023. 9:00 A.M.–7:00 P.M. Open every day.

Kimura's Antiques. Incredibly beautiful statuary.
> *Tel. (075) 561-8871. 10:00 A.M.–6:00 P.M. Open every day.*

Ezoshi Woodblock Prints. Some wonderful prints at affordable prices.
> *Tel. (075) 551-9137. 10:00 A.M.–6:00 P.M. Open every day.*

Textiles Yoshioka. Gorgeous handmade linen pillows for a (relatively) reasonable ¥12,000.
> *Tel. (075) 525-2580. 10:00 A.M.–6:00 P.M. Closed Sundays.*

Oariya. A superb range of incense starting at just a few hundred yen.
> *Tel. (075) 561-5027. 8:30 A.M.–8:45 P.M. Open every day.*

SHOPPING 119

Fancy an 1888 Biwa lute, a mere snip at ¥950,000? Or perhaps you'd prefer an 18th-century lacquerware box, depicting a scene from *The Tale of Genji,* a real bargain at just ¥6,000,000? If you haven't already gathered, the specialist antique shops of Kyoto's Shinmonzen-dori are far from cheap, but if price is no object, then this is *the* place to come for exquisite, unique, and often breathtakingly beautiful works of art. The shops lining this small street in Kyoto's Gion district each specialize in different arts. Yet you don't have to be a Rothschild or a Rockefeller to appreciate Shinmonzen-dori. All shops accept Visa, MasterCard, and American Express, which may be a mixed blessing. We suggest you start saving now.

ACCESS: A five-minute walk from either the Sanjo or Shijo stations on the Keifuku and Keihan lines, or bus nos. 12, 31, 54, 201, 202, 203, or 206 to Chionin-mae bus stop on Higashioji-dori. Shinmonzen-dori runs east to west from Higashioji-dori to Kawabata-dori, and is clearly marked in English.

Best Art Supplies

Kawachi, Osaka
Osaka-shi, Chuo-ku, Shinsaibashi-suji 1-1-8. Tel. (06) 252-5800. 10:30 A.M.–8:00 P.M., Sun. 10:30 A.M.–7:00 P.M. English spoken. All major credit cards accepted.

Everything from humble poster paints to giant canvases and busts of long-dead famous Greek fellows at this cornucopia of artist's supplies in Shinsaibashi. First floor: postcards and stationery; second floor: artist's materials; third floor: papers and canvas. For professionals and amateurs alike, they have a comprehensive selection of wares at competitive prices.

ACCESS: A three-minute walk from Shinsaibashi subway station, on the west side of the Shinsaibashi Shotengai shopping arcade, next to Sogo department store and opposite McDonald's.

Best Art Books—Japanese

Keibunsha, Kyoto
*Kyoto-shi, Sakyo-ku, Ichijoji Haraidono-machi,
10 Beru Furaru, 1F.
Tel. (075) 711-5919. 10:00 A.M.–11:00 P.M. Sun. and holidays
11:00 A.M–11:00 P.M. Open every day. All major credit cards accepted.*

A wealth of books and magazines on contemporary Japanese art and popculture can be found here. There is also a gallery and shop selling artsy-fartsy goods, candles, and postcards. Our favorite was a pocket notebook made out of beaten steel that weighed at least four pounds! This is also the best site for *tachiyomi* (reading, but not buying) in Kansai.

THE BEST OF KANSAI

ACCESS: A three-minute walk west from Eizan Tetsudo Ichijoji station on the south side of Ichijoji-dori.

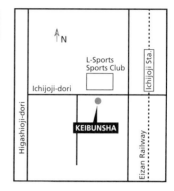

Best Art Books—Western

Librarie Arcade, Osaka
Osaka-shi, Kita-ku, Shibata 1-6-2, Hankyu Kosho no Machi 6. Tel. (06) 374-2524. 11:00 A.M.–8:00 P.M. Closed Wednesdays. All major credit cards accepted. English spoken.

Handsome European and American photo books and fine-art books can be found in this quiet, intimate bookstore. The prices are as outrageous as elsewhere, but it's a relaxing place to browse and, occasionally, splurge.

ACCESS: Chayamachi-guchi exit from Hankyu Railway's Umeda station. Beneath the railway tracks in Kosho no Machi arcade, just before you reach the Kappa Yokocho warren of small drinking alleys.

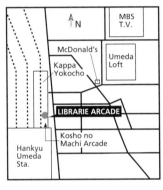

Best Beatles Memorabilia

Come Together, Osaka
Osaka-shi, Kita-ku, Shibata 1-1-3.
Tel. (06) 371-5901. 10:00 A.M.–9:00 P.M. Open every day.

Care for a Yellow Submarine ballpoint pen, filled with water, where a submarine moves back and forth as you tilt it up and down? Or a fourteen badge set proclaiming, among other things, "Love Me Do," "Please Please Me," and, er, "I am the Eggman"? Come Together holds one of the most comprehensive collections of Fab Four trivia and memorabilia this side of the Mersey tunnel. We balked at the Beatle dolls dressed in the clothes of the Sgt. Pepper album, priced at ¥165,000, and opted instead for a Working Class Hero T-shirt at a hundredth of the price. Judging by the hysterical reaction of the staff when we attempted to take photographs, we wonder how much of the merchandise is licensed, or even authentic. Could that John Lennon mobile-phone pouch possibly be a fake? Imagine!

ACCESS: In the Kiddyland complex of Hankyu Umeda station, at the foot of the escalator coming down from the Chayama-chi-guchi exit.

BEST BICYCLES BY POST

Mike's Bike Sales, Osaka Prefecture
Tel. (0726) 74-3602.
E-mail: BYP01135@niftyserve.or.jp
Cycle Craft, Osaka-fu, Takatsuki-shi, Nakagawa-cho 5-28.
11:00 A.M.–9:00 P.M. Closed Wednesdays. English spoken.
No credit cards.

Long-time Kansai resident and "cyclo-path" Mike Schultz has pedaled off into the Californian sunset, but continues his bikes-by-post business in partnership with the able fellows of Cycle Craft, Takatsuki. Since Japanese consumers balk at buying anything that is less than 110 percent perfect, Mike and his friends are able to buy machines from the factory with such heinous defects as stained tire-walls and invisibly scratched paintwork, and pass them on to foreign buyers at great prices. Used machines, too. Charley Kawatani, Ebina Shusaku, and Masaya Inoue also keenly welcome non-Japanese cyclists to join their cycle club's tours and races. Call for the latest Mike's Bike Sales newsletter.

BEST BOOKS ON OLD JAPAN

Marco Polo Books, Osaka
Osaka-shi, Kita-ku, Shibata 1-6-2, Hankyu Kosho no Machi.
Tel. (06) 374-1300. 11:00 A.M.–8:00 P.M. Closed Wednesdays.
All major credit cards accepted. English spoken.

There is no better source in Kansai for oddball Nipponalia than this tiny store nestled amid the other specialist bookshops beneath Umeda Station's Hankyu Railway tracks. The part-time staff are, well, clueless, so it's up to you to find the gems on offer here. Not so many titles, but all of them appeal. Choose from such gems as *A Diplomat's Wife in Japan, The Japanese Threat, Three Rolling Stones in Japan,* and, should you be as lucky as we were, the incredible *Yankee Hobo in the Orient.* Prices tend to start from ¥5,000, but they're always far more reasonable than those in Tokyo's Kanda Jimbocho district.

ACCESS: Chayamachi-guchi exit from Hankyu Railway's Umeda Station. Beneath the railway tracks in the Kosho no Machi arcade, just before you reach the Kappa Yokocho warren of small drinking alleys.

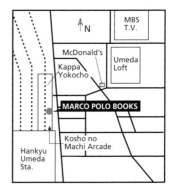

BEST COFFEE BEANS

Saga Coffee, Kyoto
Kyoto-shi, Ukyo-ku, Saga Daitokujimon-mae.
Tel. (075) 881-9282. 10:00 A.M.–10:00 P.M. Open every day. Closed January 1–5.

In the land where coffee drinking has been elevated to a fine art, we have to confess to being non-cognoscente. Until recently we thought a siphon was something you used to illegally remove gasoline from someone else's car. Yet even we can recognize that the coffee sold at Saga Coffee is something special, and the prices—two-thirds those of their rivals—make this trek to western Kyoto well worthwhile. We particularly liked the Saga

Strong Mix, a real bargain at ¥170 per 100 grams. Owner Takegami-san will give you a free cup of the day's special, but as she's somewhat loquacious, it may be best to take the beans and run.

ACCESS: In western Kyoto, on Shin-Marutamachi-dori, 100 meters east of the junction at Kiyotaki Kaido.

BEST EVERYTHING-UNDER-ONE-ROOF

Tokyu Hands, Kobe
Kobe-shi, Chuo-ku, Shimoyamate-dori 2-10-1.
Tel. (078) 321-6161. 10:00 A.M.–9:00 P.M. Irregular holidays.
English spoken. All major credit cards accepted.

Grommets? Sprockets? Gas-masks? Herring smokers? Beatles postcards? Zithers? Zimmers? Thirty-seven varieties of boomerangs? All these things and more can be found at the Kobe Sannomiya branch of this Tokyo wonderstore. The English-language store guide is both extremely helpful and unintentionally hilarious.

ACCESS: Subway to Sannomiya station. Tokyu Hands has its own exit, west 3; it's a three-minute walk north from the west exit of Hankyu Sannomiya station. Look for people carrying large, odd-shaped luggage.

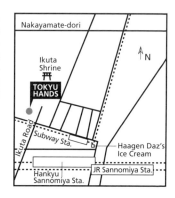

BEST EX-KIMONOS

Angel, Osaka
Osaka-shi, Chuo-ku, Higashi-Shinsaibashi 1-11-14, Nakagawa Bldg., 4F.
Tel. (06) 244-7899. Noon-9:00 P.M. Closed Tuesdays.

Claiming to be following in the traditions of the Meiji era when Japanese and Western fashion styles mixed, Angel's in-house designers produce eye-catching, chic Western-style clothes made exclusively from kimono cloth, both new and antique. The store is in traditional *gofukuya* kimono-shop style, with tatami flooring, but the atmosphere is more Katherine Hamnett than geisha girl. The place to buy that seriously cool, one-off party suit. But bring lots of cash. The hot items start at about ¥30,000.

ACCESS: On Nagahori-dori, three blocks west of Nagahoribashi station on the Sakai line subway, and four blocks east of Shinsaibashi station on the Midosuji Line.

BEST FAMILIAR DRUGS

Carewell, Kobe
Kobe-shi, Chuo-ku, Kitano-cho 1-3.
Tel. (078) 262-2510. 10:00 A.M.–10:00 P.M. Open every day.

No, not those, these are the legal kind. But if you're addicted to the vitamins, minerals, diet pills, hair-care potions, and general medicines that you used back home, Carewell is the place to find them here in Kansai. Formerly the American Pharmacy, Carewell changed its name to reflect its growing emphasis on health products rather than over-the-counter drugs. This is where we go when the late night urge for Green Algae becomes too much, or last night's excesses demand urgent Alka Seltzer.

ACCESS: In the OPA building, 1F. Subway to Shin-Kobe station or a ten-minute walk uphill from Sannomiya.

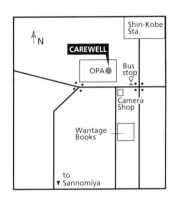

BEST FLEA MARKET

Toji Temple, Kyoto
*Kyoto-shi, Minami-ku, Kujo-cho 1.
Tel. (075) 691-3325.*

SHOPPING 131

Kyoto boasts two nationally renowned flea markets, one at Kitano Tenmangu shrine on the twenty-fifth of each month, and the other, our longtime favorite, at Toji temple on the twenty-first. The fun at Toji lies as much in the people watching as in the bargain hunting, and this is where Kyoto's kimono-clad old timers come out of the woodwork, giving the place a kind of living Taisho-era backdrop. Serious shoppers either get there early, before 8:00 A.M., or turn up around 4:00 P.M., when the last-minute haggling commences. The best bargains to be had are outside the temple grounds proper, in the streets around the north gate.

ACCESS: Kintetsu Line to Toji station, or a ten-minute walk from JR Kyoto Station's Hachijo-guchi exit. Look for the towering pagoda, or just follow the crowds.

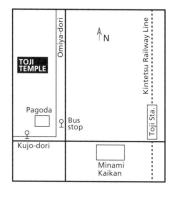

Best Free Furniture

Fukuya Furniture Company, Osaka Prefecture
Osaka-fu, Takatsuki-shi, Kyoguchi-cho 9-10.
Tel. (0726) 73-5451. Evenings; Sundays are reportedly best.

The Fukuya furniture company in Takatsuki offers to dispose of their customers' old tables, chairs, bedroom cabinets, *tansu*, etc., which they stick around the back of their retail outlet, making this a treasure hunter's paradise. They are more than happy when a hopeful foreigner turns up to cart something away.

ACCESS: Southwest corner of Hatcho-Nawate junction on Route 171.

Best Handcrafted Furniture

Hito to Ki, Kyoto
Kyoto-shi, Kita-ku, Kinugasa, Gosho no Uchi-cho 12.
Tel. (075) 462-3447 (Japanese), or (075) 751-5004 (English).
Open by appointment. Call same or previous day.

Perhaps the single largest obstacle to the runaway success of Tadaomi Inoue's woodcraft studio is that it's never open, a trifling problem which he dismisses with a big grin and a wave of his giant, calloused craftsman's hand. Thus it comes as no surprise that the two *kanji* characters of Hito to Ki, meaning "person and wood," combine to form the phrase *yasumu* (to rest). Inoue-san carves and planes and finishes his wood at his own pace, and all by hand, taking far more pride in the creation than the selling of his beautiful handcrafted furniture. While his pieces range from inexpensive items such as pens, hair clips, and lighters to small chairs and low-lying Shogi tables made of *hinoki,* the most striking and beautiful of his works are his enormous, exquisitely finished tables, wooden screens, and heavy-weight chairs, created from single pieces of wood. Expect to pay in the vicinity of ¥300,000 for a giant, outdoor seat crafted from *keyaki.* Inoue-san also creates items to order, yet sales remain a low priority. "This is just something I do when I'm not too busy," he says with a grin.

ACCESS: Hito to Ki is just a one-minute walk from the entrance to Kinkakuji temple, at the intersection of Nishioji-dori and Kuramaguchi-dori. Bus nos. 12, 59, 204, or 205 to Kinkakuji-michi.

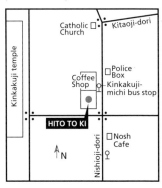

Best Handmade Shirts

Yuhei Camiceria, Kyoto

Kyoto-shi, Kita-ku, Kamigamo Sakurai-cho 65. Tel. (075) 712-1201. Mon.–Sat. 10:00 A.M.–7:00 P.M., Sun. 11:00 A.M.–8:00 P.M. Open every day. All major credit cards accepted.

Owner Nishigaki-san will make you a tailor-made shirt in two weeks from among the thousand different types of cloth he's imported from Italy, Switzerland, and Great Britain. Prices start at ¥20,000, as well they should. Kitayama chic doesn't come cheap.

ACCESS: Subway to Kitayama station. Take the exit to the rear of the train, and head west on Kitayama-dori. Opposite the Kyoto Botanical gardens.

Best Impulse Buying

Umeda Loft, Osaka
Osaka-shi, Kita-ku, Chayamachi 16-7.
Tel. (06) 359-0111. 11:00 A.M.–8:00 P.M. Open every day.
Irregular holidays.

We have seen the future of shopping and it's Umeda Loft. Or rather, we've gone to Osaka and repeatedly emptied our wallets on stuff we didn't really need. Loft is an impulse buyer's dream—or worst nightmare, depending on how you look at it—a kind of Tokyu Hands for the terminally trendy. We especially like the art supplies department and the bookstore. In the basement, Theatre Umeda features art-house movies; the gallery space on the top floor also hosts excellent exhibitions, most notably of photography. Umeda Loft is also a great one-stop shopping spot for last-minute souvenirs. On a recent visit they had at least thirty varieties of *maneki neko,* or beckoning cats, as well as Italian designer watches, antique porcelain bedpans, and more. We spent up.

ACCESS: Chayamachi-guchi exit from Hankyu Railway's Umeda Station. Loft is a three-minute walk, to the east of Kappa Yokocho, and is clearly signposted.

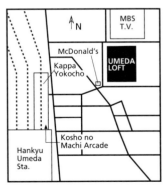

Best Japanese Paper

Morita Wagami, Kyoto
Kyoto-shi, Shimogyo-ku, Higashinotoin-dori Bukkoji Agaru. Tel. (075) 341-0123. 9:30 A.M.–5:30 P.M. Closed Sundays, holidays, and the first day of the month.

Japanese handmade paper is the finest in the world, noted for its durability as well as its beauty. Thus professional Western artists as well as Japanese calligraphers and watercolor painters head for Kyoto's Morita Wagami. The gift shop beside their warehouse sells beautiful paper fans, miniature folding screens, and the paper itself, available in myriad hues and textures from silky white to coal-tar black. Costs range from a few hundred to many thousands of yen. A catalog shows the full range of papers available.

ACCESS: Hankyu Karasuma or subway Shijo stations. On Higashinotoin-dori, two blocks south of the intersection of Shijo-dori and Higashinotoin-dori.

BEST LUXURY KITCHENWARE

Aritsugu, Kyoto
Kyoto-shi, Nakagyo-ku, Nishikikoji-dori, Gokomachi Nishi Iru.
Tel. (075) 221-1091. 9:00 A.M.–5:30 P.M. Closed Sundays and holidays.

This is the place to come if you have no qualms about spending ¥200,000 on a tofu steamer, or ¥70,000 on a knife specially devised for deboning a fish that doesn't even have a name in English. The people at Aritsugu have been selling beautifully finished, outrageously expensive kitchen equipment for four hundred years. This place is also a candidate for "Best Place for Impressing Visitors from Home with the Crazy Prices."

ACCESS: Subway and Hankyu lines to Karasuma Shijo station. A five-minute walk northwest to the rear of Daimaru department store in Nishiki Market.

BEST MAIL-ORDER EVERYTHING

Foreign Buyers' Club, Kobe
  Bookstore: *Tel. (078) 857-7944/Fax (078) 857-0559*
  General Store: *Tel. (078) 857-9001/Fax (075) 857-9005/*
  The Deli: *Tel. (078) 857-9001/Fax (075) 857-9005/*
  E-mail: fbc@majic.co.jp

Bagels, ice-cream makers, the collected works of Sartre, a kilo of cottage cheese—whatever your heart's desire, you're sure to find it at the Foreign Buyers' Club at prices far lower than you'll find in stores. Once upon a time the major drawback of the Foreign Buyers' Club was the necessity of buying in bulk, resulting in the What-on-Earth-Am-I-Going-to-Do-with-Three-Dozen-Cartons-of-Prunes syndrome. But now a bewildering array of canned foodstuffs, cheeses, etc., are available in manageable quantities from the club's General Store and Deli. We especially like their Bookstore, which will get you whatever reading material you desire in a matter of weeks, far cheaper than you'll find on offer in the specialist English-language bookstores. Membership fee ¥1,000.

BEST MALE MEMBERS

Peaches, Osaka
  Osaka-shi, Chuo-ku, Nishi-Shinsaibashi 2-10-12.
  Tel. (06) 211-1615. Noon–9:00 P.M. Sun., Mon. Noon–8:00 P.M. Open every day.

Who says the Japanese have no sense of humor? There's nothing dyed-in-the-wool about a shop that sells purple velvet elephant-shaped penis stockings. More male whatsits here than you can shake a stick at. Chocolate ones from the U.S., two-meter-tall inflatables from

Sweden, death-ray machine-gun varieties from the Planet Zog. Lots of silly condoms, too. We were amused. The teen-age girl behind the counter will sell you your jumbo glow-in-the-dark prophylactics with nary a glimmer of a smile. The lingerie shop next door is fun too.

ACCESS: On Hachiman-suji, the street that runs from Midosuji into America-mura. Walk down past the Eddie Bauer sportsclothes outlet, and Peaches is just past the shrine on the right side of the street. Listen for the giggles.

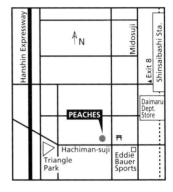

BEST MINERAL WATER

Kyoto no Shizuku, Kyoto
Kyoto-shi, Sakyo-ku, Kurama Honmachi 303.
Tel. (075) 741-3385. Fax (075) 741-2118.

Kobe's Mount Rokko water has earned nationwide fame and fortune, but we partisans of Kyoto prefer the no-frills Kyoto no Shizuku, sodium-rich water bottled in Kurama at the source of the Kuramagawa. Sizes: 1,500 ml, ¥250; 1,000 ml, ¥220; 500 ml, ¥150. Available in shops, but in Kurama just walk around the back of the factory and take what you need from the refrigerator. Payment is by the *mujin hanbai* trust system: just put your money in the box. Special hikers' bottles with carrying straps are also available, as the Tokai Shizen Hodo network of mountain trails passes right by the factory.

For those who want their water fresh from the hillside, just walk about 300 meters down the road from Kurama station, heading toward Kyoto, and you will find the Water of Life spring, Inochi no Mizu. Free—but it's polite to leave ¥5 for the gods.

ACCESS: By Eizan Railway line from Demachiyanagi to Kurama station. Kyoto no Shizuku is on the right side of the road 100 meters east of Kurama Yuki Jinja shrine.

Best Pepper

Chobunya, Kyoto
Kyoto-shi, Kamigyo-ku, Ichijo-dori, Shichihonmatsu Nishi. Tel. (075) 467-0217. 11:00 A.M.–6:00 P.M. Closed Thursdays and rainy days.

Chobunya is so tiny that you might miss it completely, were it not for the gorgeous smells drifting out onto the shopping street of Nakadachiuri-dori. Owner Uno-san grinds the *togarashi* and *sansai* and other ingredients on the spot to produce the distinctive *shichimi* seven-pepper seasoning used so widely in Japanese cooking. The small bamboo flasks of *shichimi* (¥900) make especially nice presents. Call to check that they're open if it looks like rain.

SHOPPING 141

ACCESS: Bus nos. 203 or 55, to the Kamishichiken bus stop on Imadegawa-dori, then a five-minute walk south on Shichihonmatsu-dori. Chobunya is next to the southwest corner of Shichihonmatsu and Nakadachiuri-dori.

BEST PICKLES AND GOBLINS

Watanabe Ki No Me Honpo, Kyoto
Kyoto-shi, Sakyo-ku, Kurama Hon-machi 248.
Tel. (075) 741-2025. 9:00 A.M.–5:00 P.M. Open every day. Irregular holidays.

An unlikely combination, it must be averred, but the good folks of Watanabe Ki No Me Honpo have been peddling pickled mountain vegetables and *tengu* (long-nosed goblin) masks for just about as long as anyone in the mountain village of Kurama cares to remember. The masks are exquisitely made from papier mâché, and painted either bright red or brilliant gold, and range from key-holder sized demons to enormous, white-maned, wall-sized megamonsters. We are particularly partial to the *karasutengu,* a crow goblin, who reminds us somewhat absurdly of Kermit the Frog. If mythic face wear is not your cup of tea, try the splendid pickled mountain vegetables on sale at the front of the shop. We always shamelessly eat our weight in free samples, prior to buying. The *chirimen sansho* peppers, and shiitake *shigure* mushrooms are especially recommended.

ACCESS: By Eizan Railway line from Demachiyanagi to Kurama station. Watanabe Ki No Me Honpo is on the left after you exit the station car park, just below the steps leading up to Kurama Yuki Jinja shrine.

BEST PLASTIC FOOD

Aburatani Koseido, Osaka
*Osaka-shi, Chuo-ku, Nanba Sennichimae 14-26.
Tel. (06) 641-7738. Fax (06) 633-4677. Weekdays 9:00 A.M.–
6:00 P.M., weekends and holidays 10:00 A.M.–6:00 P.M.*

A veritable cornucopia of inedibles, Koseido is the place to stock up the plastic-food replicas that adorn restaurant showcase windows, and make such popular souvenirs among our tasteless friends back home. They've got everything from single *gyoza* and pieces of sushi here, plus the more ambitious shrimp tempura and foaming glasses of beer, the legendary fork suspended in spaghetti with meat sauce, and the enormous *matsubagani* crab replicas, a mere snip at ¥25,000. Yet our favorite is the humble bowl of fermented soya beans. Even better than the real thing, as they say.

ACCESS: In Doguya-suji arcade, opposite the Central Cinema. Take the Nankai subway line to Nanba station, and walk down the Nankai-dori Arcade that is just across the street from the northeast corner of the Takashimaya department store. Turn right when you come to the Da Ole food building, past the NGK Yoshimoto Kaikan and Doguya-suji Arcade is directly in front of you.

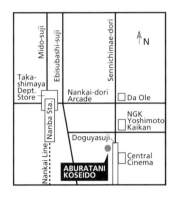

BEST SECONDHAND BOOKS

Wantage Books, Kobe
Kobe-shi, Chuo-ku, 1-13 Ikuta-cho 1-chome.
Tel. (078) 232-4516/7. Fax (078) 232-4518.
10:00 A.M.–5:30 P.M. Closed weekends.

Hankering for Hesse? Searching for a soupçon of Sartre? Or craving the latest Tom Clancy? Wantage Books (want age, geddit?) has the region's best—and cheapest—selection of secondhand books in English. Even better, the profits from the store go to support the Kansai Bangladesh Project. Books bought and sold. Upstairs are the main offices of *Kansai Time Out*.

ACCESS: Down the small side street alongside the photo processing shop diagonally opposite the OPA building. A ten-minute walk uphill from Sannomiya, or two minutes from the Shin-Kobe subway station.

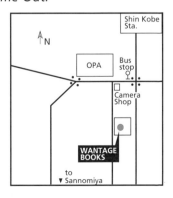

BEST SECONDHAND CAMERAS

Umeda, Osaka
Osaka-shi, Kita-ku, Umeda, Bldgs. 1, 2, 3, 4.

Not a single shop, but an area in Umeda behind the Hilton Hotel. Compare the prices and condition of equipment before you buy. Japanese secondhand camera prices are on average slightly higher than they are in the West, but the equipment itself tends to be in much better condition. Umeda Dai 1, 2, 3, and 4 buildings are the places to browse for secondhand SLRs. Some cameras that have become collectors' items, such as the Olympus OM3, are outrageously pricey, but others—the Pentax K1000, Olympus OM10, Canon AE1, and the early autofocus Canons—are real bargains. Marushin Camera in Umeda Dai-Ichi Building (Tel. 06-341-0251) seems to have especially good deals.

ACCESS: A two-minute walk to the rear of the Osaka Hilton Hotel, opposite Tower Records' Maru Biru.

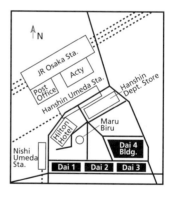

Best Secondhand Macs

Sofmap 8, Osaka
Osaka-shi, Nihombashi Denden Town, Sakai-suji, Sofmap Hachi-go Kan, 4F.
Tel. (06) 634-8844. Mon.–Sat. 11:00 A.M.–8:00 P.M. Sun. and holidays 10:00 A.M.–7:00 P.M.

Here is the place to come for secondhand Macintosh computers. Although the merchandise on display is definitely bargain-priced, everything is sold as is, with a 12-month warranty. Powerbooks start at ¥30,000. All information is in Japanese.

ACCESS: Tanimachi Line subway to Ebisucho station, exit 1A. Walk past NTT and Disk Pier. The secondhand Mac department is on the fourth floor.

Best Wine Retailer

Wine Crazy, Kyoto
Kyoto-shi, Nakagyo-ku, Nishioji Sanjo Agaru Nishigawa.
Tel. (075) 821-1208. Fax. (075) 822-0302. 9:00 A.M.–10:00 P.M. Closed Sundays and holidays. English spoken. No credit cards.

Less-than-charitable friends have suggested that our knowledge and appreciation of the grape are more akin to those of a street-dweller than a sommelier, an accusation which we refute with great ardor if little conviction as we guzzle down another bottle of Guatemalan Burgundy or Albanian Spumanti. To prove the heinous disbelievers wrong, we make frequent public appearances at Wine Crazy, western Kyoto's mecca for the serious wine aficionado. Seven years ago, owner Toshio Iwata somewhat optimistically shipped an entire building from Ishikawa prefecture, stocked his cellar with 10,000 bottles of fine wine, and opened his doors to what he hoped would be legions of Kansai fans of the grape. His gamble paid off, and today Wine Crazy is widely acknowledged as the region's finest source of excellent contemporary and vintage wines. Most of Iwata-san's customers arrive knowing what they are looking for, but he's happy to give advice—and samples—to complete ignoramuses like us. Iwata-san is quick to point out that finding an excellent wine needn't mean parting with vast sums of money. He offers a startlingly good Baron de Rothschild Sauvignon at ¥1,350, several moderately priced and currently very popular Italian reds, and a plethora of eminently drinkable French wines in the ¥2,000–¥3,000 range. However if you really want to splash out, he can offer "something in the region of ¥300,000."

ACCESS: A two-minute walk from Sanjo-guchi station on the Randen streetcar line, 100 meters north of the junction of Sanjo and Nishioji streets. Bus nos. 202, 203, or 205.

Services

BEST ADVICE—LEGAL

Kazuyuki Hori, Kyoto
 Kyoto 604, Nakagyo-ku, Tominokoji-dori Marutamachi Sagaru, Fuyu Bldg., 1F.
 Tel. (075) 241-1092.

If all goes well while you're in Japan, this service won't be necessary. Nevertheless, in matters legal there is no better advisor than Kazuyuki Hori. Well versed not only in the intricacies of his trade, but also in the specific needs and problems of Western clients, he is a sympathetic, professional legal expert. He's also extremely laid-back and friendly, the only attorney with a pierced ear and dyed hair that we've ever met. Costs vary according to each case—sometimes, he offers his services free of charge.

ACCESS: A five-minute walk east of Marutamachi subway station on Tominokoji-dori, just south of the Imperial Palace.

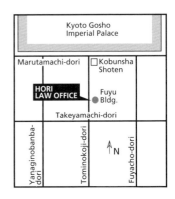

Best Cat Sitters

Cat Sitter Rusuban Neko, Kyoto
Kyoto-shi, Sakyo-ku, Yamabana Kawahara-cho 9-5.
Tel./Fax (075) 723-6514.
Internet: http://www.kyoto.nnttua.or.jp/~land/rusuneko/

Cat lovers who want to get away from home once in a while need no longer risk entrusting Tom to unreliable friends or Alcatraz-style "pet hotels." Call in pet-care advisor Hitomi Tagashira, who will pamper felines in the manner to which they have been accustomed—or most likely better than—in your own home. She will visit your house, stay an hour, feed your cat, play with it as advised, and check its health. Each time she leaves a "Cat Report." Tagashira-san insists on interviewing first-time customers and their cats, to see how each owner interacts with their pet. Prices depend on the distance she must travel from her house in northeast Kyoto, but begin at ¥2,500 per day. There is a ¥500 surcharge for more than two felines. Add 30 percent during peak holiday seasons. She will empty garbage for free, but watering the garden costs extra.

Best Change Machine

"Next-1" Department Store, Osaka
Osaka-shi, Chuo-ku, Yodoyabashi Keihan station.
Tel. (06) 227-4101. 10:30 A.M.– 20:00 P.M. Closed on third Sunday.

An unpleasant side-effect of the universally unpopular five percent consumption tax is the unnecessary amount of loose change one has to cart around. Relief is at hand thanks to the enlightened proprietors of the "Next-1" department store in the heart of Yodoyabashi's Keihan station, who have provided a machine that will change ¥1 and ¥5 shrapnel into the wholly more user-friendly ¥10 coins. Strangely enough, I've never seen anyone other than my own friends using this machine. Perhaps the citizens of Osaka find the clink of cold, hard cash reassuring?

ACCESS: Keihan Yodoyabashi station, exit/entrance 15 on the first basement floor of the "Next-1" department store.

Best Dentist

Miyazaki Shikaiin, Osaka
Osaka-shi, Kita-ku, Dojima, Hama 1-chome 2-65, Shindai Bldg., B1.
Tel. (06) 341-3234. Mon.–Fri. 9:00 A.M.–noon, and 1:00 P.M.– 5:00 P.M.; Sat. 9:00 A.M.–1:00 P.M. Closed Sundays and public holidays. Reservations necessary. English spoken.

Best Dentist may be a contradiction in terms on a par with Best Serial Killer, but when we're troubled with the occasional, to borrow a phrase from Gabriel Garcia Marquez, "bastardly molar," we head to Osaka and the wondrous anesthetic of Dr. Miyazaki.

ACCESS: Exit 7 from Yodoyabashi Subway station. Walk toward Umeda, crossing two bridges. In the basement of the Shindai Building, near Mitsubishi Bank.

BEST ENVIRONMENTALISTS

JEE, Kyoto
Kyoto-shi, Sakyo-ku, Kurodani-cho 25.
Tel. (075) 751-5404. Irregular office hours.

An excellent resource for both serious greenies and the curiously concerned. A bilingual/bicultural NGO, the Japan Environmental Exchange (JEE) acts as a kind of information clearing house for a variety of special-interest environmental groups, including the Japan Rainforest Protection Group, Gomi Project, Green English, Stop the Monju, and World Talk. JEE arranges regular talks and meetings, and has an extensive resource library of books and pamphlets in English and Japanese. Volunteers, particularly those with bilingual ability, are always needed.

SERVICES 155

ACCESS: In Kurodani, just north of Marutamachi-dori and west of Shirakawa-dori.

BEST HOME MASSAGE

Nobu-Taka Kishi, Kyoto
Kyoto-shi, Sakyo-ku, Shogoin, Nishi-machi 19.
Tel. (075) 761-8654

Been a long day at the office? Has too much temple crawling left you feeling like Quasimodo after ten rounds with Mike Tyson? Call Taka Kishi for instant rehumanization. Taka-san's golden hands are legendary in Kyoto, as is his willingness to travel to all corners of Kansai at strange times of day to minister to the cricked necks and twisted backs of stiff, stressed-out *gaijin*. One of his massage sessions makes a great—and wholly affordable—gift. For an hour of bliss, he charges just ¥5,000. Taka-san also teaches classes in shiatsu at his home in northeast Kyoto.

Best Hospital

Kyoto Miniren Dai Ni Chuo Byoin, Kyoto
Kyoto-shi, Sakyo-ku, Tanaka Asukai-cho 89. Tel. (075) 701-6111. Consultations: Mon.–Fri. 8:30 A.M.–11:30 A.M., 5:30 P.M.–7:30 P.M.; Sat. 8:30 A.M.–11:30 A.M.

Brand-new buildings, an in-house CT scan, 24-hour emergency admission, and English-speaking doctors make this private hospital in north Kyoto our favorite. Formerly known as the Yasui Byoin (locals still call it that), the hospital is quite small, with all the pluses and minuses that that entails, but we especially like the prompt consultations. Patients with or without National Health Insurance will be seen, but for long-term admission, some advance cash payment may be requested.

Kansai has a few resident non-Japanese doctors. Dr. Barraclough is a British GP, based in Kobe (Tel. 078-241-2896). In the same city, Elke Kato (Tel. 075-981-0161) is a German-born MD who specializes in Obstetrics and Gynecology at the Kobe Adventist Hospital and is available for consultations on Thursday mornings. English, German, and Japanese spoken.

ACCESS: Heading north on Higashi-oji-dori, turn right just before the second signal after the Hyakumanben intersection. Bus nos. 35, 61, or 206 to Tanaka Asukaicho.

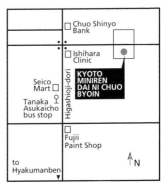

Best Human Rights Resource

Hu Rights, Osaka
Osaka-shi, Minato-ku, Benten-cho 1-2-1-1500, ORC200 Complex.
Tel. (06) 577-3578. Mon.–Fri. 9:30 A.M.–5:00 P.M. Closed weekends.

Come here to see a first-rate collection of videos, CD-roms, and two thousand books pertaining to human rights issues worldwide. Many titles are in English. Otherwise known as the Asia-Pacific Human Rights Information Center. Admission is free.

ACCESS: Chuo Line subway or JR to Bentencho station. The ORC200 Complex is immediately in front of the station.

Best Internet Service Provider

Kyoto-Inet, Kyoto
Kyoto-shi, Shimogyo-ku, Chudoji Minami-cho 17, Kyoto Kodo Gijitsu Kenkyusho Bldg.
Tel. (075) 315-9085. Fax (075) 315-2897.
E-mail: office@kyoto-inet.or.jp

A real bargain in bargain-starved Japan. Unlimited net access for ¥6,000 a year. At its worst moments, this Kyoto city government-run web service provider is busier than the Osaka loop line and slower than a Japanese baseball game, but it is by far the simplest and most economical way to get online. Membership gets you an E-mail address and telnet access, while an additional ¥3,000 provides additional addresses for family members. Heavy net users might feel it worthwhile to opt for a 64kbps ISDN digital phone line rental at ¥120,000 a year.

BEST NOSE JOB

Suzuki Jibika, Kyoto
Kyoto-shi, Kamigyo-ku, Nakadachiuri-dori, Horikawa Nishi Iru.
Tel. (075) 441-0675. 9:00 A.M.–noon and 4:30 P.M.–7:30 P.M. Sat. 9:00 A.M.–11:30 A.M. Closed Thursdays, Sundays, and holidays. English spoken.

Every spring the *sugi* (cedar) trees that ring Kyoto begin to fling out pollen, as cedar trees are wont to do, and in the process spread untold misery among thousands of *kafunsho* (hay fever) sufferers. In recent years, the pollen counts have been reaching record levels, with the *hinoki* tree adding insult to allergenic injury by flinging out its pollen a few weeks after the *sugi* have finally calmed down. Burning eyes, incessant sneezing, and an itchy throat are common symptoms of the unpleasant ailment. Fortunately, relief is at hand in the shape of Dr. Suzuki, Kansai's leading ear, nose, and throat specialist. A trip to his north Kyoto surgery is quite a cultural experience in itself. The waiting room has tatami flooring, where you sit cross-legged with fellow wheezing, sneezing, snuffling victims, before being led into a consulting room that bears a disturbing resemblance to Dr. Frankenstein's laboratory. Peculiar glass vials are attached by rubber tubing to heavy looking machinery liberally covered with mysterious knobs and dials. Fortunately, the charming Dr. Suzuki has no more sinister aims than to rid people of their distress, something he manages with considerable alacrity. On our last two visits, we had medicine blown up our noses through what looked like two inverted egg-timers, a not altogether pleasant treatment, but an incredibly effective one. The relief was almost instant.

ACCESS: Suzuki Jibika is 20 meters west of Horikawa-dori on Nakadachiuri-dori, a 15-minute walk from Imadegawa subway station. Bus nos. 9, 12, or 50 to Horikawa Nakadachiuri.

BEST TRAVEL AGENT

Time Travel, Osaka
Osaka-shi, Chuo-ku, Azuchi-machi 1-5-9, Zeniya Daini Bldg., 7F.
Tel. (06) 271-7121. Fax (06) 271-7174. Mon.–Fri. 9:30 A.M.– 6:00 P.M. Closed Saturdays, Sundays, and holidays. English spoken.

Time Travel's Sugi-san is the wonder worker of the discount-ticket world. Efficient, competitive, and a flawless speaker of English, he's also used to working out even our most convoluted itineraries. Paris via Ho Chi Minh City and Rome? The phlegmatic Sugi-san doesn't even bat an eyelid. Recently he found us a high-season plane ticket from Italy to the U.K. for a mere ¥14,000. Non-Osaka residents need not worry as all transactions may be made by phone, fax, and bank transfer.

ACCESS: A five-minute walk from exit 12 of Sakai-suji Honmachi station. Turn right out of the station, walk one block north, and turn right besides the Iwate Bank. Walk one-and-a-half blocks and the Zeniya building is on the left.

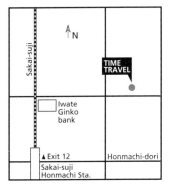

Index of Entries
and Addresses in Japanese

Restaurants

Aa Ri Shan, Kyoto (Best Budget Taiwanese)	*page* 24
亜里山　京都市下京区四条室町角 2	
Bongu, Osaka (Best Averagely Stupid Noodles)	22
凡愚　大阪市大正区泉尾町 4-4-7	
Bordeaux, Kyoto (Best Authentic French)	21
ボルドー　京都市北区大宮玄琢南町 35-5	
Cafe Zinho, Kyoto (Best Brazilian Coffee)	24
カフェ ジーニョ　京都市左京区下鴨西本町 37	
Daigin, Kyoto (Best Cheap Eats)	28
大銀　京都市左京区浄土寺東田 60	
Daruma, Kobe (Best Hida Cuisine)	34
達磨　神戸市中央区中山手通 1-16-3	
Doji House, Kyoto (Best Coffee and Dog)	30
京都市北区小山本町 20-21	
Dojo, Osaka (Best Rude Food)	41
道場本店　大阪市淀川区十三本町 1-7-4 らーざぱお1F	

INDEX OF ENTRIES

E-san, Kyoto (Best Budget Thai)   25
イーサン　京都市上京区今出川烏丸西入る今出川町 325

Furusato, Hyogo (Best Soba)   42
ふる里　兵庫県城崎郡竹野町床瀬 864

Galando, Kyoto (Best Healthy Ramen)   33
がらんど　京都市左京区田中古川町 37

Gataro, Osaka (Best Umeda Station Food)   47
大阪市北区柴田 1-7-2

Hatsuneya/Hatsune Onsen, Kyoto (Best Noodle/
  Bath Combination)   38
初音屋/初音温泉　京都市北区大山初音町 15

Homai, Kyoto (Best Traditional Chinese)   46
鳳舞　京都市北区出雲路松ノ下町 11

Ippodo, Kyoto (Best Tea—Green)   43
一保堂　京都市中京区寺町二条北

Iwaya, Hyogo (Best Wild Boar and Bath)   51
いわや　兵庫県多紀郡篠山町火打岩 495-1

Izakaya Tengu, Kyoto (Best Kyoto Station Food)   35
居酒屋天狗　京都市東山区七条通川端南下ル

Mekong, Kobe (Best Vietnamese)   48
メコン　神戸市東灘区向洋町 5-15 六甲アイランド
　マーケット シーン リバーモール ウエスト 2F

Mimi-U Honten, Osaka (Best White Rabbit Noodles)   50
美美卯　大阪市中央区平野町 4 丁目

Minden, Suita (Best Airhead Cafe)   19
ミンデン　大阪府吹田市江坂町 1-23-10 大同生命ビル 2F

Mr. Hal, Kyoto (Best Luxury Chinese)   37
京都市中京区烏丸通六角下ル烏丸プラーザ 21B1

Ninnikuya, Kobe (Best Garlic Restaurant)   32
にんにくや　神戸市中央区中山手通 2-13-1
　ランドマーク ビル神戸 5F

INDEX OF ENTRIES 163

Obanzai, Kyoto (Best Healthy Viking Lunch)   34
おばんざい　京都市中京区衣棚通御池上ル

San-kichi, Osaka (Best Okonomiyaki Internet Cafe)   39
三吉　大阪市福島区海老江 1-1-23

Tahiti, Kyoto (Best Bulldog Ramen)   26
太七　京都市上京区千本鞍馬口東入ル一筋目

Toridori, Kyoto (Best Chicken)   29
京都市上京区今出川智恵光院下ル

Tosai, Kyoto (Best Tofu Restaurant)   45
豆菜　京都市中京区蛸薬師通堺町東入ル

Yamanizushi, Kyoto (Best Rough-and-Ready Sushi)   40
やまに寿司　京都市上京区千本下立売角

Yosuko, Osaka (Best Cave Ramen)   27
揚子江　大阪市北区角田町 7-17 東宝OSMビル 1F

Yumezushi, Osaka (Best-All-You-Can-Eat Sushi)   20
夢寿司　東大阪市永田中 3-1-91 グランド メゾン樋口 1F

Sights

Darumadera, Kyoto (Best Darumas)   58
達磨寺　京都市上京区下ノ下立売通御前西入ル行衛町 457

Denden Town, Osaka (Best Nerd Watching)   73
大阪市日本橋デンデンタウン

Edo Fuzoku Hihokan, Kyoto (Best Edo-Period Erotica) 60
江戸風俗秘宝館　京都市右京区清滝村

From the TIC, Kyoto (Best Map of Kyoto and Nara)   72
京都市下京区烏丸七条下ル京都タワービル 1F

Funaoka Onsen, Kyoto (Best Bath)   57
船岡温泉　京都市北区紫野南船岡町 82-1

Gojo and Shichijo districts, Kyoto (Best Yakuza Watching)　京都市下京区五条、七条   79

INDEX OF ENTRIES

Hankyu Koku Night Sky Walk, Osaka (Best First Date) 64
阪急航空ナイト スカイ ウオーク　大阪府八尾市八尾空港 2-12 阪急航空内

Hotel California, Osaka (Best Glitz Palace) 67
ホテル カリフォーニア　大阪市中央区西心斎橋 1-9-30

Iwaya Fudo (Iwayayama Shinmyo-in), Kyoto (Best Hidden Temple) 68
岩屋山神妙院　京都市北区雲が畑

Kikokutei, Kyoto (Best Secluded Garden) 77
枳穀庭　京都市下京区下数珠屋通東本願寺

Kobe Fashion Bijutsukan, Kobe (Best Fashion Museum) 63
神戸ファッション美術館　神戸市東灘区向洋町 2-9

Mugenkyo Onsen, Kyoto (Best Hot Spring Hideaway) 69
夢幻境　鶴乃家旅館　京都府相楽郡南山城村田山 38

Museum for World Peace, Kyoto (Best Peace Museum) 74
立命館大学平和美術館　京都市北区等持院北町 56-1

Nanko Yacho Koen, Osaka (Best Day Trip from Osaka) 58
南港野鳥公園　大阪市住之江区南港北 3-5-30

Osaka Business Park, Osaka (Best International Toilets) 71
大阪市中央区城見 1-3-7

Outdoor Resort Spa Horokuyu (Kurama Onsen), Kyoto (Best Hot Water—Outdoor) 70
リゾート スパー峰麓　京都市左京区鞍馬本町 520

Panasonic Square, Osaka (Best Rainy Day Out) 76
パナソニック スクエア　大阪市中央区城見 2-1-61 ツイン 21 ナショナル タワー2F

Prinz, Kyoto (Best Photography) 75
京都市左京区田中高原町 5

INDEX OF ENTRIES

Rapi><t, Osaka (Best Back-to-the-Future Airport Train) — 56
大阪市難波南海電鉄

Ryozen-an, Kyoto (Best Early Morning Meditation) — 59
竜泉庵　京都市北区紫野大徳寺町 107

Sanzen-in, Kyoto (Best Tourist Temple) — 78
三千院　京都市左京区大原来迎院 540

Shinbashi, Gion, and Pontocho districts, Kyoto (Best Geisha Watching) — 65
京都市新橋、祇園、先斗町

Tanta Sekiyu, Kyoto (Best Giants Gas Station) — 66
丹田石油　京都市北区紫野西野 60

Tawaraya Ryokan, Kyoto (Best Sleep) — 77
俵屋旅館　京都市中京区麩屋町通 姉小路上ル

Tourist Information Center (TIC), Kyoto (Best Advice—Tourist) — 55
京都市下京区烏丸七条下ル京都 タワー ビル 1F

Bars

Hachimonjiya, Kyoto (Best Shutterbug Bar) — 92
八文字屋　京都市中京区木屋町通四条上ル大西ビル 3F

Jam House, Kyoto (Best Metalhead Bar) — 88
京都市下京区木屋町四条下ル 250 m

Kimura Sakaten, Kyoto (Best Classic Stand-up Boozer) — 85
木村酒店　京都市上京区出町通桝形上ル

Kotobuki Shuzo, Osaka (Best Microbrewery) — 89
寿酒造　大阪府高槻市富田町 3-26-12

Matera, Osaka (Best Cozy Late-Night Cocktails) — 87
大阪市中央区東心斎橋 2-8-21 日宝畳屋町会館 3F

Mekhong, Kyoto (Best Candlelit Nightcap) — 84
メコン　京都市北区西鴨水垣町 79

166 INDEX OF ENTRIES

O Bar Osaka, Osaka (Best Bourbon with a Bite)   83
大阪市中央区南船場 4-4-8 クリエイティブ心斎橋 7F

Post Coitus, Kyoto (Best-Named Bar)   90
京都市左京区田中飛鳥井町 45-2

Rasta King, Kyoto (Best Reggae Cave Izakaya)   91
ラスタ キング　京都市中京区木屋町三条下ル山崎町 245
　クラリオン ビル 5F

Entertainment

Barajujikan, Kyoto (Best Whips and Chains)   114
薔薇十字館　京都市中京区高瀬川角四条上ル木屋町 367

Cine Friends Nishijin, Kyoto (Best Gay Cinema)   104
シネ フレンズ西陣　京都市上京区千本通 西陣京極東入ル

Cinema Verite, Osaka (Best French Movies)   103
大阪市北区堂山町 5-9 扇会館 B1

Diva, Osaka (Best Tunes)   111
大阪市中央区東心斎橋 1-17-15 丸清ビル 6F

Fureai Sports Daigo, Kyoto (Best Aaaargh!)   97
ふれあい スポーツ醍醐　京都市伏見区桃山町山ノ下 19-6

Japan Foundation, Kyoto (Best Free Movies)   102
京都市中京区烏丸錦上ル安田火災海上ビル 8F

Jugglin' Rink City, Osaka (Best Reggae Warehouse)   109
ジャグリン りんく シテイ　大阪府泉佐野市りんく
　往来南りんく パーク内

Kansai Time Out, Kobe (Best What's On)   113
神戸市中央区 1-13 生田町 1 丁目

Kurama Hi-Matsuri, Kyoto (Best Fire Festival)   101
鞍馬火祭　京都市左京区鞍馬由岐神社

Kyoto Connection, Kyoto (Best Stand-Up-and-Do-Your-Thing)   110
京都市北区紫竹栗栖町朝倉ビル 2F

INDEX OF ENTRIES   167

Kyoto Ticketshop, Kyoto (Best Discount Tickets) 京都 チケット ショップ　京都市上京区笹屋町千本西 　笹屋町 4-304-7	99
Masaaki "Elvis" Takakura, Kyoto (Best Elvis) まさあき エルビス 高倉　ライブハウス ナッシュビル 　京都市中京区御前通 四条下ル	100
Minami Kaikan, Kyoto (Best Cinema) みなみ会館　京都市南区西九条東比永城町 78	98
Nichibunken, Kyoto (Best Library) 日文研　京都市西京区御陵大枝山 3-2	105
Orochi, Osaka (Best Oops Upside Your Head) 大阪府吹田市千里万博公園 1-1 Expoland	107
Padou, Osaka (Best Place to Shoot Your Friends) 大阪市西区千代崎 3 丁目北 2	108
Taku-Taku, Kyoto (Best Live House) 磔磔　京都市下京区富の小路仏光寺下ル	106
Video Station, Kyoto (Best Video Rental) 京都市左京区百万遍交差点上ル百万石ビル 1F	112

Shopping

Aburatani Koseido, Osaka (Best Plastic Food) 油谷高正堂　大阪市中央区難波千日前 14-26	143
Angel, Osaka (Best Ex-Kimonos) エンジェル　大阪市中央区東心斎橋 1-11-14 　ナカガワ ビル 4F	128
Aritsugu, Kyoto (Best Luxury Kitchenware) 有次　京都市中京区錦小路通御幸町西入ル	137
Carewell, Kobe (Best Familiar Drugs) ケアウエル　神戸市中央区北野町 1-3	129
Chobunya, Kyoto (Best Pepper) 長文屋　京都市上京区一条通七本松西	140

INDEX OF ENTRIES

Come Together, Osaka (Best Beatles Memorabilia) 大阪市北区柴田 1-1-3	124
Foreign Buyers' Club, Kobe (Best Mail-Order Everything) 神戸市東灘区向洋中 1-14-203	138
Fukuya Furniture Company, Takatsuki (Best Free Furniture) 福屋家具　大阪府高槻市京口町 9-10 　国道 171 号線八丁畷交差点南西角	132
Hito to Ki, Kyoto (Best Handcrafted Furniture) 人と木　京都市北区衣笠御所ノ内町 12	132
Kawachi, Osaka (Best Art Supplies) カワチ　大阪市中央区西心斎橋筋 1-1-8	120
Keibunsha, Kyoto (Best Art Books—Japanese) 恵文社　京都市左京区一乗寺払殿町 10 ベルフラール 1F	121
Kyoto no Shizuku, Kyoto (Best Mineral Water) 京都の雫　京都市左京区鞍馬本町 303	139
Librarie Arcade, Osaka (Best Art Books—Western) 大阪市北区芝田阪急古書のまち 6	123
Marco Polo Books, Osaka (Best Books on Old Japan) 大阪市北区芝田阪急古書のまち 1-6-2	125
Mike's Bike Sales, Osaka (Best Bicycles by Post) 大阪府高槻市中川町 5-28	125
Morita Wagami, Kyoto (Best Japanese Paper) 森田倭紙　京都市下京区東洞院通仏光寺上ル	136
Peaches, Osaka (Best Male Members) 大阪市中央区西心斎橋 2-10-12	139
Saga Coffee, Kyoto (Best Coffee Beans) 嵯峨コーヒー　京都市右京区嵯峨大徳寺門前	126
Shinmonzen Dori, Kyoto (Best Antique Street) 京都市東山区新門前通	117

INDEX OF ENTRIES 169

Sofmap 8, Osaka (Best Secondhand Macs) 146
ソフマップ 8　大阪市日本橋 でんでん タウン 堺筋
　ソフマップ 8 号館 4F

Toji temple, Kyoto (Best Flea Market) 130
東寺　京都市南区九条町 1

Tokyu Hands, Kobe (Best Everything-Under-
　One-Roof) 127
東急ハンズ　神戸市中央区下山手通 2-10-1

Umeda, Osaka (Best Secondhand Cameras) 145
大阪北区梅田第 1、第 2、第 3、第 4 ビル

Umeda Loft, Osaka (Best Impulse Buying) 134
梅田ロフト大阪　大阪市北区茶屋町 16-7

Wantage Books, Kobe (Best Secondhand Books) 144
神戸市中央区 1-13 生田町 1 丁目

Watanabe Ki No Me Honpo, Kyoto (Best Pickles and
　Goblins) 142
渡辺木ノ芽本舗　京都市左京区鞍馬本町 248

Wine Crazy, Kyoto (Best Wine Retailer) 146
わいんくれーじ　京都市中京区西大路三条上ル西側

Yuhei Cemiceria, Kyoto (Best Handmade Shirts) 134
ユウヘイ Camiceria　京都市北区上鴨桜井町 65

Services

Cat Sitter Rusuban, Kyoto (Best Cat Sitters) 152
留守番猫　京都市左京区山端川原町 9-5

Hu Rights, Osaka (Best Human Rights Resource) 157
大阪市港区弁天町 1-2-1-1500 ORC 200 Complex

JEE, Kyoto (Best Environmentalists) 154
京都市左京区黒谷町 25

Kazuyuki Hori, Kyoto (Best Advice—Legal) 151
堀和幸法律事務所　京都市中京区富小路丸太町下ル富友ビル

INDEX OF ENTRIES

Kyoto-Inet, Kyoto (Best Internet Service Provider)   157
京都市下京区中堂寺南町 17 京都高度技術研究所ビル

Kyoto Miniren Dai Ni Chuo Byoin, Kyoto (Best Hospital)   156
京都民医連第二中央病院　京都市左京区田中飛鳥井町 89

Miyazaki Shikaiin, Osaka (Best Dentist)   153
宮崎歯科医院　大阪市北区堂島浜 1 丁目 2-65 新ダイビルB1

"Next-1" Department Store, Osaka (Best Change Machine)   153
大阪市中央区京阪淀屋橋駅内

Nobu-Taka Kishi, Kyoto (Best Home Massage)   155
岸　信隆　京都市左京区聖護院西町 19

Suzuki Jibika, Kyoto (Best Nose Job)   158
鈴木耳鼻科　京都市上京区中立売通堀川西入ル

Time Travel, Osaka (Best Travel Agent)   159
タイム トラベル 大阪　大阪市中央区安土町 1-5-9 銭屋第 2 ビル 7F

Index by City

Kyoto Area

Kyoto City: Central

Aa Ri Shan, 24
Aritsugu, 137
Barajujikan, 114
Hachimonjiya, 92
Hori Horitsu Jimusho, 151
Ippodo, 43
Jam House, 88
Japan Foundation, 102
JEE, 154
Kyoto-Inet, 157
Morita Wagami, 136
Mr. Hal, 37
Obanzai, 34
Rasta King, 91
Shimbashi, Gion, and Pontocho, 65
Shinmonzen Dori, 117
Taku-Taku, 106
Tawaraya Ryokan, 77
Tosai, 45

Kyoto City: North

Bordeaux, 21
Cafe Zinho, 24
Cat Sitter Rusuban Neko, 152
Doji House, 30
Hatsuneya/Hatsune Onsen, 38
Homai, 46
Kimura Sakaten, 85
Kurama Hi-Matsuri, 101

Kyoto Connection, 110
Kyoto no Shizuku, 139
Mekhong, 84
Resort Spa Horokuyu, 70
Sanzen-in, 78
Watanabe Ki No Me Honpo, 142
Yuhei Camiceria, 134

Kyoto City: Northeast

Daigin, 28
Galando, 33
Keibunsha, 121
Kyoto Miniren Daini Chuo Byoin, 156
Nobu-Taka Kishi, 155
Post Coitus, 90
Prinz, 75
Video Station, 112

Kyoto City: Northwest

Chobunya, 140
Cine Friends Nishijin, 104
E-san, 25
Funaoka Onsen, 57
Hito to Ki, 132
Iwayayama Shimyoin, 68
Kyoto Ticketshop, 99
Museum for World Peace, 74
Ryozen-an, 59
Suzuki Jibika, 158
Tahiti, 26
Tanta Sekiyu, 66
Toridori, 29
Yamanizushi, 40

Kyoto City: South and Southeast

Fureai Sports Daigo, 97
Gojo and Shichijo district, 79
Izakaya Tengu, 35
Kikokutei, 77
Minami Kaikan, 98
TIC, 55, 72
Toji Temple, 130

Kyoto City: West

Darumadera, 58
Edo Fuzoku Hihokan, 60
Masaaki 'Elvis' Takakura, 100
Nichibunken, 105
Saga Coffee, 126
Wine Crazy, 146

Rural Kyoto Prefecture

Mugenkyo Onsen, 69

Osaka Area

Higashi Osaka City

Yumezushi, 20

Osaka City: North Central
(Umeda, Sonezaki, Kyobashi, Yodoyabashi)

Cinema Verite, 103
Come Together, 124
Dojo, 41
Gataro, 47
IMP, 71
Librarie Arcade, 123
Marco Polo Books, 125
Miyazaki Shikaiin, 153
Next-1, 153
Osaka Business Park, 71
Panasonic Square, 76
San-kichi, 39
Time Travel, 159
Umeda Dai 1, 2, 3 & 4 buildings, 145
Umeda Loft, 134
Yosuko, 27

Osaka City: South Central
(Honmachi, Shinsaibashi, Namba, Nihombashi)

Aburatani Koseido, 143
Angel, 128
Denden Town, 73
Diva, 111
Hotel California, 67
Kawachi, 120
Matera, 87
Mimi-U Honten, 50
O Bar Osaka, 83
Peaches, 139
Rapi><t, 56
Sofmap 8, 146

Osaka City: Southwest
(Taisho-ku, Nanko, Benten -cho)

Bongu, 22
Hu Rights, 157
Nanko Yacho Koen, 58
Padou, 108

Osaka City: Suburbs

Izumi-sano City

Jugglin' Rink City, 109

Suita City

Minden, 19 Orochi, 107

Takatsuki City

Fukuya Furniture Co., 132 Mike's Bike Sales, 125
Kotobuki Shuzo, 89

Yao City

Hankyu Koku Night Sky Walk, 64

Kobe Area

Kobe: Central

Carewell, 129 Ninniku-ya, 32
Daruma, 34 Tokyu Hands, 127
Foreign Buyers' Club, 138 Wantage Books, 144
Kansai Time Out, 113

Kobe: Rokko Island

Kobe Fashion Bijutsukan, 63 Mekong, 48

Rural Hyogo Prefecture

Furusato, 42 Iwaya, 51